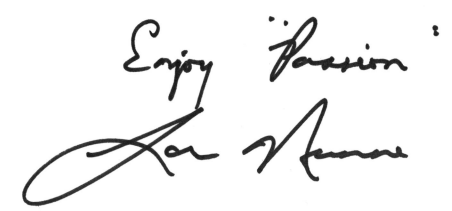

Enjoy "Passion"

A Passion to Win

A Passion to Win

Lou Nanne
with Jim Bruton

TRIUMPH
BOOKS

Triumph Books and colophon are registered trademarks of Random House, Inc.

Library of Congress Cataloging-in-Publication Data
Nanne, Lou, 1941-
    A passion to win / Lou Nanne with Jim Bruton.
      p. cm.
    ISBN 978-1-60078-368-5
    1. Nanne, Lou, 1941– 2. Hockey Players—United States—Biography.
I. Bruton, James H., 1945– II. Title.
    GV848.5.N36A3 2010
    796.962092—dc22
    [B]   2010031770

This book is available in quantity at special discounts for your group or organization. For further information, contact:

Triumph Books
542 South Dearborn Street
Suite 750
Chicago, Illinois 60605
(312) 939-3330
Fax (312) 663-3557
www.triumphbooks.com

Printed in U.S.A.
ISBN: 978-1-60078-368-5
Design by Sue Knopf
Photos courtesy of the author unless otherwise noted

To my family,

who have made my life

heaven on earth

Contents

Foreword

Having been involved in hockey for most of my life, I am humbled and deeply honored to write the foreword for Lou Nanne's autobiography, *A Passion to Win*. Never has a book title been more fitting, and never has there been a professional athlete more deserving of telling his story.

Lou is one of the most interesting and dynamic human beings I have ever met. His life has been full of incredible stories, humorous escapades, and worldly encounters that few people ever experience.

Our first meeting goes back almost 50 years, when I was putting together a team from the United States to play some games in the Soviet Union. From the very first time we met, there has been a special bond and mutual admiration between us. It has lasted more than five decades.

Whatever Lou tackles, he takes on at the speed of 100 miles per hour. He is relentless and never lets up until the task is accomplished. He has a story to tell. There are few professional athletes who can claim to have been a player, coach, general manager, and president of a professional sports franchise. And since leaving professional hockey, Lou has engineered a magnificent career in the financial industry. And he still maintains an unceasing desire to assist and promote in the development of the elite hockey athlete for U.S. Olympic competition.

In addition, as a member of the USA Hockey Foundation, he has provided relentless support and efforts toward the continuing betterment of hockey in the United States.

Lou Nanne's memoir is a fascinating story that takes the reader through his entire life, from the streets of Sault Ste. Marie, Ontario, to the University of Minnesota, the U.S. Olympic Team, the Minnesota North Stars, and into the world of finance. This book is filled with incredible stories and wonderful anecdotal memories as Lou takes us along on his incredible odyssey.

The book is brilliantly entertaining, filled with incredible recollections of Lou's experiences in hockey and in life. This is a story about a man who for the first time shares his deeply ingrained passions, most heartfelt sorrows, and emotional beliefs. It is a story of a man who has lived his life to the fullest and, in the process, has made a remarkable difference in the lives of others and for the wonderful game of hockey at all its levels. Lou shares with us his great passion for winning and doing the right thing above anything else. He shares his devotion to his family and his penchant for success in hockey and in the business world.

Travel with Lou as I have on his journey through life. It is a magnificent trek. I'm glad he took me with him.

—*Walter L. Bush Jr., chairman of USA Hockey
and former president of the Minnesota North Stars*

Foreword

What a terrific honor to contribute to *A Passion to Win*, the autobiography of my longtime friend Lou Nanne. If 100 people had the opportunity to know Lou as I do, none of the 100 would like him—they would all *love* him! When Lou walks into a room, he lights it up like fireworks on the Fourth of July.

My best description of this remarkable man can be summed up in a few words: "Cream doesn't rise to the top; it works its way up." You will never find an individual who works harder than Lou Nanne. He wants to win and be successful at everything he does. There is no compromise. And for the past 50 years, he has proven that hard work, dedication, and commitment will get you there.

I first met Lou in the mid-1960s. I had heard good things about him at the University of Minnesota and wanted him to come to work for me, selling envelopes. I am very proud that my evaluation of Lou as a potential sales superstar was proven by him in spades. To this day I have not encountered another young person with a more impressive prospect for a sales career than Lou. Hiring him was one of the best business (and personal) decisions of my life.

Selling is very competitive, and to operate a successful business, a top-notch sales force is essential. To Lou, second is last. If he calls on

100 prospects, he believes he will achieve 100 sales. Anything less would be a disappointment. Lou not only goes full speed ahead to run over his competition, but he stops, goes in reverse, and runs over them again to be sure they aren't wiggling. He is ferocious, totally focused.

Lou Nanne has had a marvelous and fascinating career, beginning as a hockey star at the University of Minnesota, then moving to the U.S. Olympic Team; the Minnesota North Stars as a player, coach, GM, and president; and now in financial management. He could have been a success at anything he tried. Knowing my close friend for the past five decades, I have found Lou to be several things. He is a super salesman with a great sense of humor. He is passionate, competitive, an incomparable storyteller, inspiring, and confident. As a mentor, coach, and business executive, Lou is a sterling example of integrity, credibility, honesty, and great compassion. He sets the bar high for himself. Lou has a wonderful gift for living life well and sharing it with everyone in his path. Perhaps his greatest trait is that he never treats another person in a way that makes one feel less important.

I have great passion for University of Minnesota Gopher football. Whenever I fly to out-of-town games with Lou and friends, we always wonder en route why we spend so much time listening to a broken-down hockey player explain the game of football to us, but we do. Lou is incredibly smart and entertaining.

A Passion to Win follows Lou Nanne from the ice arenas to the television and radio airwaves and through the financial world and brings him into our hearts and souls. This is the story of an incredible human being that was waiting to be told. His journey from the streets of Sault Ste. Marie, Ontario, to where he is today is now literally an open book, detailing many great stories, wonderful anecdotes, and heartfelt memories. His journey stands second to only one other thing in his life: the love he has for his family.

In his autobiography, Lou Nanne brings the reader with him through all of the engaging aspects of his life in a heartwarming and inspirational fashion. I hope you allow him to bring you along. I promise a great ride.

—*Harvey Mackay*

Introduction

They call him "Sweet Lou from the Soo" and he is the most recognized name in Minnesota hockey. He played in 635 regular-season games in the NHL, all of them for the Minnesota North Stars. He led the WCHA in scoring—*as a defenseman*—and was the captain of the Minnesota Gophers and the U.S. Olympic Team.

Lou Nanne has done it all. He had a magnificent career in hockey, winning All-American honors at the university and earning unprecedented credentials with the Minnesota North Stars as a player, coach, general manager, and president. In addition, his unwavering support of USA Hockey has been exemplary.

Following more than three decades in hockey at the collegiate and professional levels, Nanne has become successful in the world of finance and built a second career in the past 20 years in the money management business. His reputation in hockey and in business sets a standard worthy of the highest esteem. His value system, built on operating with honesty, integrity, and credibility, has been a hallmark of his character.

Nanne has had a brilliant and distinguished career. He is recognized for his leadership and burning desire to win. Most who know him and have been around the game for a long time will say he is the most competitive person they have ever met.

In a career spanning more than 50 years of organized hockey, he has been an inspiration to others, both on and off the ice. His passion and endless desire to win a Stanley Cup Championship as the general manager of the Minnesota North Stars eventually led to him leaving the game he loved. When the intensity became too great to bear and the desire to win rose to the forefront of his life, he stepped away for good.

Nanne is one of the most colorful and interesting personalities of the modern sports era. He has countless stories and amazing anecdotal memories associated with hockey and his personal life. He has brought to the state and region 46 years of color commentary and game analysis for the Minnesota State Boys High School Hockey Tournament.

This book is the story of an American icon whose intensity for the game burns as strong today as it ever has. He shares incredible stories and memories of his youth in "the Soo," at the University of Minnesota, with the Olympic Team, the North Stars, and beyond. But this is not a book about hockey or a former hockey player. It is a book about Lou Nanne, whose drive and "passion to win" exemplify his very being. That passion permeates every aspect of his life. This is a book about a man who has become a legendary force in the world of amateur and professional hockey, someone who has touched the hearts and souls of those who have entered his arena.

—*Jim Bruton*

Acknowledgments

If you asked me what the word *life* means, I would tell you family, friends, and experiences. That's what this book is about, and that's why writing this part is so easy.

First, to my wife, Francine. She has traveled this path with me for 48 years and has experienced much of it with me. She has been loving, hardworking, conscientious, and magnificent through it all. She has been our family's backbone.

We have been blessed with four children—Michelle, Michael, Marc, and Marty—who never cease to give us pleasure and love, and who have made our life a heaven on earth. Then they married Tino, Sheila, Lisa, and Patti, who are the perfect spouses. No one could have complemented each of them more.

To our grandchildren Bianca, Vinni, Megan, Shawn, Erin, Lauren, Anthony, Matthew, Michael, Louie, and Tyler, who have enriched our lives beyond comprehension.

To my sister Julia, brother Michael, and their families—the Nannes, Rebellatos, and all of the Grecos—who have lived these stories with me.

To all my friends and former teammates who have made my life so thrilling and exciting. You are too many to name but you know who you are.

To my assistant, Terry Magnuson, for her help with the compiling and editing of this book. And finally, but very importantly, to Jim Bruton. He convinced me to do this and then was patient, thoughtful, and open to all my changes.

I hope that it's as interesting, informative, and enjoyable for you along the way as it has been for me. However, I want you to know, I'm not ready to go just yet.

1

From "the Soo" to the U

"Louie, you're late again! Look what time it is!"
"Yeah, but Mom, I got 12 goals!"
"Okay, then," she said.

It was that way quite often. I was always playing sports—during the day, late in the evening, on the weekends, in the summer, fall, and all year round. Sports are about all I can remember.

I grew up in Sault Ste. Marie. "The Soo" is a small steel town on St. Mary's River in northern Ontario, Canada—the third largest city in Northern Ontario, with a population today of 75,000. Just to the south is the United States and Sault Ste. Marie, Michigan, the cities being joined by an international bridge connecting Interstate 75 in the U.S. and Huron Street in Canada.

We lived on the west end of the city, about two blocks from the steel plant, which was the largest local employer. My mom owned a small clothing store that was across the street from my dad's grocery store. The grocery was originally owned by my mother's father. Mom operated her store with her sister, and her sister's husband partnered with my dad at the grocery store. The two stores were every bit family businesses. And the Nannes and the Rebellatos were inseparable.

We lived with my father's parents, and with both Mom and Dad working long hours at the stores, we had to make sure we occupied ourselves during the day, and we did a pretty good job of it—playing sports from early morning until late at night most every day of the year. In the summer it was baseball, in the winter we played hockey, and we filled the rest of the time with football, tennis, and basketball—and in between, hockey again in the streets.

Our house sat on Allen Street with about 14 others on the block. The homes were very close together and you could cut the grass with nail clippers. Three of the houses were owned by bootleggers, women whose husbands had died, which made for an interesting entrepreneurial environment in the mid-1940s. Many of us lived with other family members. And *everybody* had a nickname. There was "Ma Shaw" Verdone, "Munna" Maniacco, Jimmy "Putsa" Piromalli, "Chachi" Longarini, Carlo "Schmutzie" Longarini, "Pepper Nose" Sanzosti, "Turkey" Archangeletti, "Beansie" Rossi, "Fatty" DiPasquale, and "All Pants" Greco.

Most of the city of 40,000 people was made up of Italian or part-Italian families with some French, Fins, and the occasional German, British, Scotch, and Irish. There was also a Polish section of the city. But overall, they say more than 20,000 had some Italian in their lineage.

Sault St. Marie was a strong hockey community, and I was not excepted. My passion for sports began before I was old enough to be on any kind of an organized school team. I was as young as five years old when I started. We played most of the sports on our neighborhood block or at St. Mary's or the McFadden schoolyard.

When we were growing up, my cousin Jimmy and I used to play catch in the lane with Mike "Zetsa" Scarfone beside Zetsa's house. The biggest bootlegger in the West End, Jimmy Vena, lived in the apartment above the house. Any time the police would raid him, Mike's mom would tap on the wall in a certain spot to tip him off, and Vena's crew would put the whiskey on a dumbwaiter that was hidden behind a false closet and lower it inside the house.

One day we were throwing the ball around when the police stormed the place, attempting a surprise raid. They ran upstairs with their axes to break down the door, but were surprised to find steel behind the wood. They put ladders up to the side of the building, but as they got to the windows, they found bars on them. I was amazed how well fortified Vena's place was. He wasn't about to get busted.

My passion for sports seemed to grow by the day and hockey rose to the top of the list. It didn't matter what time of the year it was. If I had a stick in my hand, I was happy. There was only one indoor ice-skating rink in town—and it was closed in the summer—so we played baseball and fast-pitch softball. But for most of us, hockey reigned supreme. We couldn't wait to get back onto the ice.

In my day, the Soo Greyhounds—the senior team—was the most notable in the area. As a young boy, I dreamed of playing for them. The team has existed since the formation of the Northern Ontario Hockey Association in 1919, and it has been the fantasy of most young hockey players to someday play for the Greyhounds. They remain incredibly popular as a Junior A team today.

Sault Ste. Marie was approximately 360 miles from the National Hockey League city of Detroit, Michigan, so the Detroit Red Wings were my favorite team. I remember listening to the games on the radio. And on Saturday nights, with just about every other Canadian kid, we listened to Foster Hewitt, who brought us the action of the Toronto Maple Leafs. He was the most recognized Canadian hockey broadcaster, and for many years he was the premier hockey play-by-play man for *Hockey Night in Canada*. He also is given credit for the famous hockey phrase, "He shoots, he scores!"

I remember sitting and listening intently to the radio as he started off every broadcast with his memorable, "Hello, Canada, and hockey fans in the United States and Newfoundland." Even now, when I think of the sound of his voice, I still get the chills.

Hockey names from those decades-ago broadcasts are cemented in my memory. Players like Ted Kennedy, Syl Apps, and Turk Broda, the former Maple Leafs goaltender who led Toronto to three Stanley Cups from 1947 to 1949. And even though I recall so many of those famous Toronto names that came across the airwaves, I remained a true and loyal fan of the Detroit Red Wings. They were my team. Gordie Howe was my ultimate hero, but I loved all of the Red Wings.

Howe started his career in 1946, about the same time as I started following professional hockey. He was one of the most dominant forces in hockey history. To me, it seemed like he had played forever.

In 1953 I was 12 years old and had the opportunity to meet Gordie Howe. Marty Pavelich, who played for the Red Wings, is from Sault Ste. Marie and coached our summer baseball team. Howe came to our field to visit Pavelich. I was really involved in hockey in addition to baseball, so Marty wanted to introduce us. It was an unbelievable moment in my life. Whenever I think about it, it seems like it took place yesterday.

"This is Lou Nanne," I remember Marty telling Howe. "He loves to play hockey here in the Soo and is a huge Red Wings fan." I can still visualize Gordie putting out his giant hand to shake mine. I looked at the size of his wrist and forearm—it looked like one solid piece of steel! It was incredible. I will never forget that day—now close to 60 years ago—and how I felt meeting the great Gordie Howe. It was one of the defining moments of my youth.

Howe was friendly and so engaging to all of us kids on the baseball team. I remember that he had such a great smile—a stark contrast to his on-ice persona. It struck me that he had a Jekyll and Hyde personality.

As I got to know Gordie personally some years later, I found him to be one of the nicest, kindest, most soft-spoken people anyone could ever want to meet. But playing hockey he was a completely different person—mean, tough, and so incredibly competitive. He would never let anyone stand in the way of him winning a game. He would crush an opponent in an instant in order to prevail.

I always compared him to the great "Rocket" Richard of the Montreal Canadiens. Both of them were so nice in person; on the ice, a completely different story. Ted Lindsay was the same way. He is a terrific person out of uniform, but in a game he was as tough as they come—mean, dirty, tenacious, and willing to go to any lengths to win. The passion and intensity that these players brought to the game was amazing. I have such respect for each of them and have idolized them throughout my life.

When I was growing up, I wore No. 7 because I loved Terry Biocchi, who played for the Sault Ste. Marie Greyhounds. Terry was a tremendous player on the senior team and I used get a thrill when I saw him in church on occasion. As a youngster, players like Howe and Biocchi were such stars, it was almost as though they existed only in our imagination, so when we actually saw them it was unbelievable.

I never would have dared to dream I could be like Gordie Howe or play in the National Hockey League; I would never have let those dreams get that far out of hand. I hoped I would be able to someday be good enough to play for the senior team like Terry Biocchi. For all of us growing up, that was our ultimate dream. The senior team was our entire focus. It was all I thought about when we played hockey in the streets and later when I attended St. Mary's School.

When I was 10, I was on the school team playing for St. Mary's as a peewee. I was always the team captain and in charge of changing up the lines during games, so at my young age, I would let my thoughts drift from time to time and actually think about playing professional hockey in the National Hockey League. But it was only reverie. It just didn't seem realistic.

By the time I reached 14 I was immersed in hockey, playing as much as possible and listening to the NHL games on the radio. As I listened to Al Nagler do the Red Wings games I let my dreams run rampant. I remember the broadcasts were always brought to us by Stroh's Beer.

And then on Saturday nights it was Foster Hewitt and *Hockey Night in Canada*. I wasn't really into reading the newspaper sports pages then, so I got almost all of my hockey information from the radio. There were only the original six NHL franchises, and I pretty much knew what was going on with all the teams in the league.

There was a great rivalry that existed back then between the Montreal Canadiens and my Detroit Red Wings. And even though I always wanted the Red Wings to win, I admired the great "Rocket" Richard of Montreal. He was such a dynamic player, who played the game with such intensity and was a hero across all of Canada.

In those days I spent so much of my time listening and hearing about the great players of our era, but I had no idea I was playing in the streets with future hockey legends. Phil and Tony Esposito were friends and neighborhood boys. (Of course, both turned out to become Hall of Fame players in the National Hockey League.) I also played with Chico Maki, Gene Ubriaco, and Matt Ravlich.

In our house we had no television, so everything to us was playing sports. We played hockey right in front of our house if the schoolyards had games going on. We attracted kids from all over the neighborhood to our imaginary arena, and usually 6 to 12 of them showed up for games.

Our street hockey games were very competitive. I wanted to win every time we played; losing even a street hockey game was not an option for me. Sometimes our team would be behind at quitting time and I would insist that we play longer so we had an opportunity to come back.

As I mentioned, my local heroes were those who played on the senior team, the Sault Ste. Marie Greyhounds. During our street games I used to let myself dream on occasion but then would set myself straight, thinking, *How could I ever be good enough to play for the senior team?*

I mentioned that I liked to pretend I was Gordie Howe, but I also liked to imagine that I was "Red" Kelly of the Red Wings. I was enamored with Kelly because he was a defenseman and I really enjoyed defense. His real name is Leonard Patrick Kelly and he was sometimes known as the player who played on more Stanley Cup–winning teams (eight, in his case) than any player who never played for the Montreal Canadiens. Even today when I see Red, my thoughts drift back to my youth and how much I wanted to be like him.

I later learned that Kelly had also grown up listening to the radio broadcasts of Foster Hewitt, and that he was given the inspiration to play as a defenseman because of the hard-charging style of Toronto Maple Leafs defenseman Red Horner, as described by Hewitt.

Red Kelly was a great player for Detroit and a real hero of mine. He had the distinction of winning the first Norris Trophy, awarded to the league's best defenseman, in 1954. I have never forgotten that a Toronto Maple Leafs scout once recommended that the team pass on Kelly as a projected player; the scout believed he didn't have the ability to last even 20 games in the National Hockey League. After all, Kelly played for the Red Wings from 1946 to 1960 and then the Maple Leafs from 1960 to 1967. So he only played about 21 years past the predicted 20 days! I always wondered if that brilliant assessment of talent cost the scout his job.

It would be unique and special to me that I pretended to be some of the NHL's greatest players and then later in life played against them and became friends with them. I actually had the opportunity to play against Gordie Howe. Of course, Howe played professional hockey for 35 years—with Omaha, Detroit, Harford, Houston, New England, and the Detroit Vipers. He had a magnificent hockey career and retired when he was 52.

Even though I was loyal to the Red Wings, I was enamored by the teams in Montreal, Toronto, Chicago, Boston, and New York and all of the great talent each of them had. I was mesmerized by the games, the players, and the action. I absolutely loved every aspect of the game.

Since Detroit was close to home, I had the opportunity to take the ferry across to Sault Ste. Marie, Michigan, to watch the Red Wings at training camp. They always trained there at Polar Stadium, and in September my family and I would go watch them practice. It was incredible. There they were, the Detroit Red Wings, right there with us! The experience brought me even closer to the game and stoked the fire within me.

I recall one afternoon after practice, I got a ride back to the Canadian side from Leo Reise and Metro Prystai. There I was, nine years old, riding in a car with two Detroit Red Wings players. It was unbelievable. They all knew I was from the Canadian side, since I had attended their practice a few days in a row and had taken the opportunity to talk with several players.

I did a lot of things to satisfy my hunger for sports at a very young age, as a matter of fact. I can't even imagine my grandkids doing some of the things I did during those years. Besides having a great love for hockey, the Detroit Tigers were also an obsession. I used to marvel at the likes of Al Kaline, Harvey Kuenn, George Kell, and so many others.

When I was six, my Aunt Babe and Uncle Nick, who lived in Detroit, brought me to see the Tigers play the Boston Red Sox. I remember it perfectly. It was my first major league game. During the game Ted Williams came to bat and my Uncle Nick turned to me and said that Williams loved to hit the ball to right field around Section 36. Sure enough, on the first pitch Williams hit one off the facing of the second deck—right by Section 36.

After that, I was hooked. I went to Detroit every summer to see them play from the ripe old age of nine until I was 20 years old. I would catch the Greyhound bus at 10:00 PM and ride the 365 miles to Detroit alone. I would always seem to get the same bus driver every year and I sat right behind him on the trip. His name was Wendell Sheppard and he always kind of looked out for me. We would cross the Mackinaw Bridge late at night and it was so dark and foreboding. When we got to the ferry and all the passengers debarked and went upstairs, I stayed right there next to Wendell. I never let him out of my sight.

We would arrive in Birmingham, Michigan, about 7:00 AM and Uncle Nick would be there to pick me up. Mom would give me $35 to take along—with a very specific charge. I had to buy gifts for my brother, sister, cousins, and other relatives. My aunt would always take me to Hudson's Department Store and I would fill up on socks and candy, anything to stay within the $35 and still accommodate the family.

But my main purpose in going was always to see the Tigers play. I would get to see two to three games during the week I was there. But I was always left wondering why my aunt didn't let me go more often. I wanted to go every day.

By the time I was 12, I would take the streetcar to the ballpark by myself and hang around the dugout between games during double-headers. I really enjoyed talking to the players. I remember Reno Bertoia gave me an autographed baseball. I told him I was Canadian and Italian like he was. I thought that because of our connection he might give me something, like a baseball, and he did.

When I wasn't involved in sports—which was pretty much all the time—my friends and I found other fun things to do. The train came within about 100 yards of our house so we often jumped on it, rode for a while, then jumped off and walked back. During the winter we would grab onto car bumpers, crouch down so the driver didn't see us, and slide along on the streets to the movie theater and back. Whenever we did something that got us in trouble, we would take off over the rooftops. The houses in the neighborhood were close enough together that jumping from one to the next was not a problem. We did a lot of crazy things but always had a good time.

St. Mary's Grade School was one block from my house. The principal was a nun and a strict disciplinarian. We always had a student from the eighth grade in charge of the bell to dismiss the class for recess and lunch. One day, when I was the bell ringer, the Sister left the room for a second and I put the clock on her desk ahead one hour. When it reached noon, I rang the bell and let the whole school out. The kids now had two hours and 20 minutes for lunch instead of an hour and 20. It didn't take her long to find out I was the culprit. Suffice it to say, I never got to be the bell ringer again. I had a mischievous streak that I wrestled with for a few years. Nothing major, but I loved to pull pranks.

I always tried to emulate my sports heroes but also I liked cowboys. My favorite was the Durango Kid. Once I tried one of the Kid's great stunts. I climbed the roof at Stan Fera's house and waited for one of my friends to come by so I could jump off the roof on him, like the

Durango Kid would do when he nabbed a bad guy. I jumped, but I missed and landed right on my stomach. The fall knocked the wind out of me and I was the laughingstock of the neighborhood that day.

My friends and I used to attend wrestling matches at the Memorial Gardens. Yukon Eric, Don "One-Man Gang" Evans, and Rufus Jones were among our favorites. Following those bouts, we would go and wrestle in my basement. There was a wine room off to the side, where my grandfather and dad stored barrels of wine. Unfortunately, one day one of us forgot to fully close the spigot after having a taste, and we lost a few gallons of wine. My grandfather wasn't a happy camper.

In addition to street hockey, I played organized hockey at all levels. There were grade school teams, bantams, midgets, and juveniles and the competition was fierce at every level. I found success and began to think that I might be able to play further, perhaps even professionally someday. Usually though, I would rid myself of the thought quickly.

Phil Esposito and I grew up together and remain friends. Phil was a terrific player and got better and better as he matured. He became one of the greatest scorers of all time.

Phil actually didn't play junior hockey until he was 19 years old; by comparison, Bobby Orr was in juniors at the age of 14. Phil had great hands and was a fantastic stick handler and an uncanny scorer. When he was in Chicago and playing on the same line as Bobby Hull and Chico Maki, he was absolutely unbelievable. Like his brother Tony, Phil was a great athlete. He was one of those players who could literally slow the game

"Louie could have been anything he wanted to be in life and he would have been very successful at it. He is one of the real fun people in life. He makes me laugh all the time. We have been friends for over 60 years."

—PHIL ESPOSITO, LONGTIME FRIEND

down for himself, hold out until the last second possible, and then put the puck in the net. That phenomenal trait in the great ones allows them to "play the game from the press box." The higher up you go in the stadium the more the game slows down and the easier it gets to play.

Tony was a goaltender and an exceptional player. He was also an outstanding running back in football, and Phil was a good player too. I was involved in baseball, fast-pitch softball, and basketball. We all just loved sports and the competition that went with it. I loved the challenges, the intensity of the games, and the passion surrounding everything about sports. But most of all I liked winning—and I got used to it.

We also had contests in the Boy Scouts. Once we had a contest to see who could sell the most apples. I had my dad drive me to the Greyhounds games at the Memorial Gardens, because I knew three to four thousand people would be attending. I would set up shop at the front entrance and sell enough to win. Italian people love young dandelions called *chicottia*. Occasionally, I would go to the parks or find some manicured lawns and fill a number of baskets. I would sell them for one dollar each. It was a nice way to make a little money.

But then I enjoyed winning at everything. I remember when I was in grade school, we would have memory contests in class. I would study and practice so that I could be the one who memorized the most lines in the class.

When I was 12, I recall that we used to have hockey races at St. Mary's School. We would line up and race each other. On one occasion, a kid beat me, and I came second. I can still remember the song being played during the race: "I've Got a Lovely Bunch of Coconuts." It was my one loss in all those races in grade school and I still remember it. I am 69 years old and to this day losing that race still bothers me.

Most of the guys from our neighborhood were pretty talented hockey players. Every year we would win the championship, no matter what level we were playing. In fact, it eventually got to the point where we would win so often that the majority of the fans who filled the arena for the championship game of Ontario would be rooting against us, just to see the underdog win. It didn't bother me; as far as I was concerned winning was the only thing that mattered.

I had an overwhelming desire to win even in those street hockey games and as I got older the intensity level became even stronger. I never wanted to lose a game at anything. It didn't matter the sport, the time of the year, or the game, I wanted to win.

When there was ice on the streets we used pucks, otherwise we used tennis balls. We would pack up snow to serve as makeshift goals. The games were very competitive; aggressive is too mild a term to describe the action. I got hit in the shins a lot with the puck and smacked with a stick plenty. There was a great deal of body-checking in our street games and sometimes even fighting. But the bottom line for me was always winning. It was all that mattered for me, but we still had such great fun in the process.

On one of our juvenile teams we had a player by the name of Red DePaulo, who got his nickname because of his long red hair. We also used to call him "Peckerhead." One Sunday afternoon a midget team was playing a game. The linesman was a short, bald-headed guy by the name of Dinzmoor. I'll never forget that game and what Dinzmoor did to me. And all because of a little misunderstanding.

During the game, I picked up the puck and was moving up the ice with Red. We were making a rush into their zone. I had the puck and Red had gone offside, killing our attack. Dinzmoor blew the whistle. I was upset and hollered over at Red, "What are you doing, Peckerhead?" Dinzmoor thought I was talking to him for blowing the whistle and gave me a 10-minute misconduct penalty for calling him "Peckerhead."

I yelled at him, "No, no, I'm talking to my friend, Red. We call him Peckerhead!" Dinzmoor says, "No you're not, you called me a peckerhead," and he put me in the penalty box for 10 minutes!

After the game, Red's mother came up to me and said, "You know, Louie, maybe you guys ought to call Red something else besides Peckerhead." We never called him that again.

During those years, I was always one of the smallest players on the team, and I usually played as a defenseman. Depending on the game, if it was close at the end, I might be moved up to forward. In bantams, most of my teammates outweighed me by 20 pounds, but I was still effective because I developed a bucket check that was basically a hip check. I became fairly skilled at it and really held my own on the ice during our games. At the time there was a player by the name of Harry "Bucket Check" Taylor who played for the Sault Ste. Marie Greyhounds. I used to watch how he made the check and then copied him when I could.

At my size, if I had tried to hit someone head on, it just wouldn't have worked, so I used the bucket check until I got bigger. Once during our team playoffs, I recall hitting a kid who outweighed me by 60 pounds with the check and flipping him right over. I thought, *Wow, this works perfectly. No use getting steamrolled by the big boys.*

I also learned how to block shots, a crucial defensive skill. Joey Bumbacco taught me how to do it and I studied his technique seriously. He had the ability and technique to teach it and I learned it well.

When blocking shots, don't leave your feet unless you are in front of the net. If you do, the shooter can fake a shot and go around you. You need to go down on one knee, keeping your stick held away from you. When you do it the right way and you block the shot, the puck will often come out ahead of you, giving the opportunity for a breakaway. I had a few breakaways in my career when I played forward. When you are closer to the net, you can leave your feet to block the shot and smother it. But you have to make sure to block it, otherwise the goalie will be screened and hard-pressed to stop it. I look at players today and there are very few who really know how and when to block shots properly and yet this defensive technique is such an important part of the game.

One year in peewees, we were playing for St. Mary's School in the city championship game. Since we didn't have a coach, as team captain I was also the coach and in charge of changing up the lines during the game. The game seemed to go on forever with no score. Finally Jimmy Sanko, a player for the other team, scored and they beat us. I will never forget it. It was the only time we didn't win the championship in the next seven years. It was one of our few losses.

Both Sanko and I had good opportunities throughout the game to score. We were back and forth up the ice and I felt I would be the one who did it. I was 11 years old at the time, and I still remember every minute of the game. I can still see Jimmy scoring that winning goal. And to this day, I can't shake it. The losses and disappointments stay with me forever. I wish we could play the game again.

Growing up and worshipping the greats of the game was easy for me because I loved hockey so much. I recall what a great team the Montreal Canadiens were, and with Richard as their focal point it was hard not to think of them as the best team. But Detroit was my team, and in my mind Gordie Howe was better than the "Rocket" because he was a Red Wing, not a Canadien. I was actually obsessed with this. Once I convinced myself that Howe was better, I was comfortable with everything. I know that sounds crazy, but I had to do it or I would be troubled by the thought.

Richard played for the Canadiens from 1942 to 1960 and was the most prolific goal scorer in the 1940s and 1950s. He was the first to score 50 goals in a single season, a feat most thought was impossible. He was also the first player to score 500 goals in his career. While Maurice Richard was in Montreal playing for the Canadiens, they won the Stanley Cup an incredible eight times. And though I worked it out in my mind that Howe was better, I knew how great a player Richard was.

I have so many incredible memories listening to hockey games on the radio, especially once the Stanley Cup playoffs began each year. The excitement of the playoffs and all the pressure and intensity that went with them fascinated me, and it was a huge part of my life every spring.

In the early 1950s I badly wanted the Boston Bruins to beat the Canadiens in the Cup finals, and I was so disappointed when Richard scored on Bruins goaltender "Sugar" Jim Henry to win it for Montreal.

Typically, if the Red Wings were out of it, I rooted for Boston— but they could never seem to get over the hump. They had the great "Kraut Line": Milt Schmidt, Woody Dumart, and Bobby Bauer. They were all fantastic players. The amazing thing about those guys is that they played together in junior hockey and were childhood friends before they went on to become professional teammates.

Schmidt was a tremendous center for the Bruins, a great stick handler and wonderful playmaker. He, Dumart, and Bauer stayed together with the Bruins for almost 15 seasons. He later became the coach of the Boston Bruins. Milt Schmidt became general manager of the Boston Bruins and stayed in the organization for years. When I think back on those moments, I feel like a kid again engulfed in that great hockey lore of the past.

The Chicago Blackhawks were another of the original teams in the National Hockey League. They owned the rights to players on the Sault Ste. Marie Greyhounds. Much like the Bruins and the New York

Rangers, the Blackhawks never seemed to be able to get their act together. They were typically at the bottom of the heap, while the Toronto Maple Leafs, the Red Wings, and the Canadiens were on top. I always thought that the Blackhawks acted as if they were the farm team of the Red Wings, because Detroit always seemed to end up with Chicago's best players. Of course, that was okay with me, because the better the Red Wings were the happier I was, but it seemed unusual that it worked out that way.

When I was 13 years old, Chicago owned my rights as a player because they sponsored our team. Everyone who played on our team in the Soo was owned by Chicago, and they had the players' rights for a future in professional hockey.

There was no draft back then. NHL teams would sponsor clubs across Canada and keep an eye out for talented players. If they thought you could move up to Junior A, you would have to play for a sponsored team. Once a franchise had you sign a "C" form, you were theirs.

The Blackhawks had come into the Soo and worked out a deal many years before with our manager, Angelo Bumbacco. They gave us money for team uniforms and equipment, claiming ownership rights of the players in return.

At that time, there was no high school hockey being played in the Soo. We played bantams and our rights were with Chicago. In actuality, it was because of this system that I ended up going to school at the University of Minnesota and playing college hockey for the Gophers.

My mom and dad wanted me to attend college and go to dental school. My plan was to go to the University of Toronto and play for St. Mike's, but the Blackhawks would not let me do it. "No, no, no," Rudy Pilous of Chicago told me, "You are going to go to McMaster in Hamilton. We'll get you a car and you can play for St. Catherine's, the team associated with the Blackhawks."

But I didn't want to go to McMaster because they did not have a dental school. Chicago told me that I could go to dental school later and told me they were not going to allow me to go to Toronto and play for St. Mike's. Dictating my hockey life was one thing, but I was not going to let them tell me what I was going to do for my career. I was very stubborn, as they found out. The Blackhawks actually owned my rights for professional hockey from the time I was 13 years old and would until I was 26—but I never played for them. I was not going to go to college for four years and then start dental school, and that was that. It was not going to happen. We were both stubborn and I would say that in the end, I won out.

There was no question at the time that I had my differences with Chicago. They just weren't a franchise that I liked. And frankly, most of us in the neighborhood didn't like the Toronto Maple Leafs either. We always felt they had a prejudice against Italians because they didn't have any for a long period of time. I don't know how purposeful it was, but we felt it was.

Things were really different back then. Players' rights were owned by the established NHL franchises for years, and there were only six teams. And within the rosters of those six teams were few American players, even though four of the NHL cities were in the United States. Every now and then there would be a Brimsek, Karakas, or Mariucci, but they were few and far between.

It was a difficult time trying to decide what to do and to some extent, being strong-armed by the Blackhawks played a part. In the end it all worked out just fine. I am the type of person, even back then, who analyzes situations and then makes the most informed decision possible. And once I make up my mind, my stubborn nature comes out—especially when someone tells me I can't do what I want to do.

When we were 10 to 12 years of age, most of us in the neighborhood played hockey for St. Mary's. When we weren't playing at the schoolyard, we were back in the streets. I also worked as the stick boy for the senior team. I gathered the broken sticks. Then I'd nail them back together so that we all had sticks for street hockey. I had more sticks than you could imagine, and everyone would get one if they needed it.

By the time we were 13, Phil was playing with us. I recall our neighbor, Joe Merolini, who lived across the street. He worked the late shift at the steel plant, so he wanted to sleep during the day. If we were making too much noise, he would call the police, who would confiscate our sticks if they caught us, so when we saw them coming we often had to run down the street. But overall they were kind to us. They would ask us to break up the game, but in a half hour or so we went right back at it. We never lost too many sticks to them.

I honestly cannot remember a day when I was not playing hockey. From October until April we would play in the streets after school and then after supper, we would go to the rinks where we could skate. The local rinks were used for public skating from 4:00 PM to 6:00 PM everyday so we had to wait until early evening to use them. We would practice shooting against the garage door, and nailed two pucks together to make them heavier and harder to shoot. We would have a little contest by picking the spot on the door and continually trying to hit it.

The equipment we used was pretty primitive compared to what is used today, but we survived. My folks could afford to help me out somewhat because of the stores they operated but for the most part all we needed on the streets were hockey gloves. It was there that I got my first set of stitches. It took seven of them to close the wound. I took a blow to the face from an errant hockey stick. It would the first of more than 320 stitches that I would take in the face before my hockey career was over. I like to say that actually "I stopped counting after 320 stitches."

I can remember my dad once telling me, "Louie, I am so tired of taking you to the doctor to get stitches. If you get cut again, don't you come home!"

That very night I went out to play at dusk. We were playing hide-and-seek, not even playing hockey—and I was running full speed toward a garage door that I *thought* was raised. It was down. I ran right into it and I got a large cut on my head. So much for fair warning.

My dad was a great guy. He was the very best in the world. When I was a senior in high school, I needed a new pair of skates. I went to my mom first and asked her if she could help me out with a new pair of "tacks." I told her they cost $92. Mom looked me in the eye and said, "Louie, that's too much money! Forget it. You are going to school to be a dentist. You don't need a pair of skates that cost that much!" I said, "But Mom, I really need these skates and if you buy me a pair I am going to get a scholarship to play hockey at school so you won't have to pay the money for me to go to college." She didn't budge one inch. "Louie," she said, "We will find the money for you to go to school. Give up this hockey."

I went to my grandmother next and convinced her I needed them. I asked her to please talk to my dad about it and she did. Dad thought about it for a while and finally was convinced that it was important for me to get the skates and he came up with the money.

My grandfather sided with Mom on the issue. He had a little trouble with the English language and the pronunciation of some words but we all knew what he meant. "Louie," he said to me, "You know what the trouble with you is, mystery?" He couldn't pronounce "mister." "You need your reducation. That's right, you need your reducation." I knew he really meant education. He said, "Forget sport, you need your reducation!"

Even though we lived with my dad's parents, we all got along very well. Dad had his grocery store, mom ran her clothing store, my grandfather had a construction company, and my grandma took care of the house. We had a great family and a good life together. We were all very close and we were also closely connected to our extended family. Mom and Dad truly appreciated family values and that has carried over through generations.

Mom was a tough lady, an extremely hard worker who had her ideas about things. Like me, she was very set in her ways. She was an amazing person. She was very kind and caring and was very smart. And every one of my friends knew not to get on her bad side.

Every Friday night after work and supper, she would bake. I'm sure that a lot of women in our neighborhood did some baking from time to time, but I know for sure no one did it like my mom.

She would close the store at 6:00 in the evening on Friday, come home from work and eat dinner and then head downstairs to start baking for the family. Every Friday night she would do the same thing. And did she bake! She was from a family of 10 so she really knew what was needed with my brother and sister, my mom and dad, and both grandparents all together in the same house. She would go to my dad's store at closing and take all the spotted fruit. She was very creative. Have you ever had a peach/apple/rhubarb/blueberry pie? Each piece that you cut is different.

Many a Friday night she would be up until 2:00 AM baking away in the basement. And she wasn't just baking to provide for us in the house. It was for her brothers' and sisters' families as well. She also fed all the kids who came to our house after Mass on Sundays. This was their treat before we played street hockey. Though if someone missed Mass they didn't get any.

Her schedule was often: close the store, come home and eat dinner, bake until 2:00 in the morning, get up at 6:00 AM, bake until 9:00, go and open up the store Saturday morning, before repeating everything again Saturday night.

Our church was directly behind our house about 100 yards away. Mom went to church every day and when the priest lost his house-keeper, Mom had him eat at our house. She was that way. She was always helping people out in any way that she could.

In addition to all Mom did for others, she would also spend time visiting the hospitals. She would visit people that she didn't even know. She always felt that the people who were in the hospital who didn't have any visitors needed company, so she would go and see them. On the way she would make a stop at Dad's grocery store and bring the patients fruit. And if she knew they didn't have the proper clothing to wear, she would make a stop at her clothing store and provide them with clothes too. As I mentioned, she was an amazing woman with a wonderful gift of kindness.

Mom was also unafraid to tell it like it is. I remember once I took her to Interlachen Country Club for dinner and we happened to be seated next to some friends of mine, Chuck Pohlad and his wife, Sandy. After dinner Chuck came over and asked me to introduce him to my mom. He looked at Mom and said to her, "Mrs. Nanne, I am so glad to meet you. You are such a beautiful woman." Mom looked directly at Chuck and said to him, "I do have a mirror at home." Then she walked away.

I said to her, "Mom, why do you have to say things like that? Chuck was trying to be nice to you."

"Louie," she said simply, "I have a mirror and I know what I look like." That was Mom.

When I was being recruited in high school, I got a call from the hockey coach, Ned Harkness at RPI in upstate New York. As we talked on the phone, it came up that I had mostly A's on my transcript but not in a physics class. He asked me if there was a chance I could get the grade changed to an A so it would look better, since RPI was an engineering school. Mom overheard the conversation and said, "Louie, you hang up the phone right now, you don't go to a school where they are not honest!" She was as honest a person as the day is long. She would not tolerate anyone who wasn't honest.

When it came to operating the store, Mom was tough. She expected people who purchased items to pay their bills and she would often go to their home to get her money when they didn't pay. When I was 16, she had me go out and do some of the collecting for her. But she was also understanding. She only collected from people she knew had the ability to pay. If someone didn't have the money and came into the store, she would give them what they needed. She was very perceptive to people's needs and never gave a thought to helping out someone who needed it.

Mom taught me to be fair to people and to be honest. She probably had more influence on me businesswise than my dad. She was a sharp businesswoman and really taught me what was important in that respect. Both Mom and Dad taught me about money. "Don't ever owe anybody anything, Louie," Dad would tell me. "You always pay your own way, and if someone gives you something, you always return the favor." Mom and Dad both felt very strongly about this. They were both hard workers and always paid their own way. They were very proud people and this was very important to them.

Friday was always payday at the steel plant, which was two blocks from their stores. Right down the street sat two pool halls. One was owned by Norman "Sockeye" Ciotti and the other by Dolly Sarlo. It was not uncommon for some of the workers who worked the night shift to head right to the pool halls with their paychecks. And it was not uncommon for some to gamble away all their money. Then they would come into Dad's store broke and in need of food for their families. "I have no money but I will pay you later," they would tell my dad, and he always would accommodate them. "Sure, it's okay. What do you need?" Dad would ask.

It used to bother me that he did that. I can recall saying, "Dad these guys work all week, get off work in the morning with their paychecks, and they go to the pool halls and blow all their money. And then they come to you and want food for free. Why do you give it to them?"

Dad said to me, "Louie, these guys work hard. If they need help you have got to give it to them. Don't worry about it. One day they will pay it back to us." Unfortunately, many never did.

When Dad died in 1975, he had $7,500 on the books still owed to the store. He had more money owed to him than he had cash in the bank. But it was his way. As I look back and saw the way he did things, it makes me proud of him. He was a kind-hearted person and, like Mom, would always help someone in need.

When I was playing midgets and juvenile hockey, I used to get off the bus from school and stop into the store and tell Dad that I needed a steak for my pregame meal. The butcher shop was in the back of the store. Dad would take me to the cooler, slice off a nice piece of meat and I would take it home for my grandmother to cook for me. It was always a fantastic steak and I loved those meals. They were so good that I thought about telling him I had more games than really were scheduled. I couldn't get enough of those steaks.

My mom and dad rarely saw me play hockey; they were always working. Dad was a fan but he worked seven days a week. The store was open six days and then before church on Sunday he was usually at work stocking shelves for the coming week. He never had the time to take off and come to games.

I remember that he came to a bantam game at Central Park. (The park has now been named Esposito Park after Tony and Phil.) Most of our games were played there until we became midgets and played at the Memorial Gardens. He and my mother also saw me play the Oshawa Generals for All-Ontario Championship. They were sitting with my girlfriend Francine, when I caught a skate above the eye. As I left the ice, bleeding profusely, my dad got up to check on me. My mom grabbed him and said, "Where are you going, Mike? You're no doctor. Sit down and let him handle it." He also saw me play a few times in college when we came to play at Michigan Tech. He would come to the games there and he was able to see me play six times against Tech.

Mom was rarely able to get to the games. She never saw me play for the Gophers or with the U.S. Olympic Team, and she never saw me play in the National Hockey League. But she did watch the games on television when they were on in my hometown.

Even though Mom never attended the games, there was never any lack of interest in what I was doing. She was always on top of what was going on. She had her store and she was working all the time. And on the weekends, she was baking. That's just the way it was and the way she was. Her goal and dream for me was not in hockey but in dental school. Above all else, she wanted me to be a dentist.

I truly wanted to go to dental school and make a career out of dentistry but I had a sense that I really wouldn't enjoy it. I had two quarters in dental school before I transferred to business school.

I figured this out rather quickly after dissecting a frog the first time. After I pulled the pins out, the frog jumped right out of the pan. I knew at that moment I was in the wrong vocation. No more biology classes for me. I had to change my course of direction and do it quickly. That was it. The next day I went over and took interest tests at the "U." I had the highest interest in sales that my guidance counselor had ever seen. Business school, here I come.

One of the toughest things that I ever had to do in my life was to tell my parents I quit dental school. My mom's brother was a dentist and had been very successful and she wanted that for me as well. He had a cabin, a nice car, a big boat, and she knew I could become a partner with him someday. She wanted a good life for me and she saw that in dentistry. I guess she understood that the frog and I were not going to make it together. However, my parents did get their dentist. My brother, Michael, went to McGill, got his dental degree, and came back to Sault Ste. Marie to practice. My son, Michael, also became a dentist, as did my sister's two girls, Bridget and Joanna.

When I was away at college, my mom wrote me a letter every day. It meant a lot to me that with all she was involved with in her life, she found the time to write to me every day. She would tell me what was going on at home and kept me up to date on everything happening back at "the Soo." I called home once a week and would write letters home once in a while too. And every March, Dad would give me his car to drive back so I had a car at school for the spring quarter.

Dad taught us to work hard, be thoughtful, and be kind. I always knew that my parents were proud of what I accomplished even though they never talked much about it. We had a relative who was somewhat successful and did a lot of boasting about it.

"We don't want to be like that, Louie," Mom would tell me. "When you are successful, people will know about you. You don't have to talk about it." I know she was proud of all my hockey accomplishments. But if you talked to her, you wouldn't think I ever did anything besides go to school. And she was exactly the same with my sister and my brother.

She was a strict disciplinarian. She would never under any circumstances allow us to be late for anything. And if you were late, there would be a price to pay for it. Even today, I am never late. Never! And my kids will tell you that we raised them the same way, because being punctual shows respect for the people you're meeting.

When I was older, I would try to talk my parents into going on a vacation somewhere, but they never went anywhere. They were very content to stay in Sault Ste. Marie. Our family has a cabin a few miles from home on the St. Mary's River and my parents would say, "This is our vacation."

I did the same with our kids growing up. During school break every year, they would come to me and ask, "Where are we going on vacation this year?" They always heard the same thing from me. "We are from the Soo. That's where you are from. We stay home during school break, just like the kids from the Soo."

When my daughter was in high school she came to me and asked if she could have a car. I told her, "No you can't have a car, you are from the Soo and you don't get a car in high school when you are from the Soo." It was our value system and I carried it on in our family.

I lost both my mom and dad at early ages. Dad was only 58 years old when he died. He had developed Hodgkin's disease, and when the city took his store as a part of urban renewal, it had a profound effect upon him. He was very troubled by that, and I always felt that made his health worsen.

When my dad became ill, I owned a farm in Litchfield, Minnesota, and I wanted my parents to come and live there. I thought it would work out well for them and Dad could go to work as a butcher in town. It would allow him to keep busy and likely make him feel better. I was hopeful they would accept my offer and then they would be close to my family.

But they would have no part of it. I recall Mom saying to me, "Are you crazy? We're from 'the Soo.' We will stay here. All of our family is here. We will be okay." But things were really tough on them. Dad had nothing going on and the stress that he was under was very hard on him. He died in 1975, the day after my birthday.

Dad was such a hard worker and a great provider for our family. Little things he said to me stuck in my head. One day when I was 13 years old, I was leaving the house to go out and he said to me, "Louie, do you have any money in your pocket?" I told him no. Dad said, "Here, take this $5. You don't go anywhere without money. Always pay your own way, Louie." I have never forgotten that conversation with him.

He would also say, "Dress like a man, be neat and clean." Many times he would work all day at the store from 6:00 in the morning until 6:00 at night, come home from work, take a shower, and put on a suit and tie for supper. Then after we ate he would go out and walk around the neighborhood, all dressed up. When I was 11 he took me to the men's store in town and bought me a new suit. He always thought it was important to look sharp. "There you are, Louie," I recall him saying. "You really look sharp."

Dad had a presence about him. He liked nice clothes, enjoyed a good cigar and new cars, and was a very level-headed, easygoing person. He really enjoyed people. He was just a very kind-hearted man. People knew him, liked him, and respected him.

Dad and I used to deliver groceries to his customers all over the city and I often made the trips for him. I recall driving six miles each way to deliver a 30-cent pack of cigarettes to a lady. "Oh, Louie," she said. "It was so nice of you to drive way out here to deliver this for me." I told her that if it were up to me I wouldn't have done it, that it was my dad's doing. But that was my dad. He took care of everyone. If someone needed something and he was able to provide it for them, he did it.

There is no question that my dad had obsessive-compulsive disorder, which is most likely why I have it. He had all the signs and symptoms. I remember some of the crazy things he would do. We would be locking up the store at night and he would lock the door and open it, lock the door and open it, lock the door and open it. He might do it 15 times before we left and went home. Mom used to say to him, "Mike, what are you doing? I am going to strangle you. When the door is locked, it is locked." But he would do it anyway. He could be sitting at a desk and he would tap one side and then the other side, then two times on one side and two times on the other side, then back and forth. It was absolutely nuts. Now I do the same thing.

I mentioned their vacations were always to our cabin, which was just a few miles away. There are four cabins in a row, and all of them were family owned. I couldn't convince my parents to take a trip to New York or any other place. It was tradition, pure and simple. And to this day every single Sunday the Greco and Nanne families are together for lunch. Men bring homemade wine, the women do the cooking, and it is an enjoyable day. It's all about family. Maybe 30–60 people show up. This happens every Sunday in summertime and has been going on for more than 50 years. It was and continues to be a family tradition.

Because I grew up going to our cabin with my family, I decided that my family should have one too. My teammate Ted Harris and I were talking about it after practice one day, and Ted suggested I buy a farm. He told me that kids like farms and animals, and said they would have more fun there. It made good sense to me, but I still wanted to be on water. I was fortunate to buy a farm on a lake in Litchfield, Minnesota. The family had a wonderful time enjoying the horses and cows, as well as the lake. I loved it too, except for one bad experience.

My wife, Francine, wanted a garden, so I set out to make her one. I went all out. I planned it to be about 25 feet by 15 feet. She told me that I was going to need a rototiller. I said, "What's that?" She said I would need it to churn up the ground. So I went into town and rented it from the hardware store. They showed me how to get it started and I thought, *This is going to be easy.*

Boy, was I wrong. After two hours working that machine, I had had it. My hands had blisters and were throbbing. I was in misery. That was when Cesare Maniago and his family stopped by our farm. He came over and looked at my progress and said, "Let me try it." He got nowhere for 10 minutes. I told him I was going to get this thing working and went to push the machine again. As I did, my hand slipped down the shaft and hit this lever that was sticking out. Suddenly the machine started to churn the ground. I worked our garden plot for two hours with the —— thing in neutral. I should have remembered what my dad told me years before: "Work hard so that you can hire someone to do the things that you aren't capable of performing and know nothing about."

I don't think I would have made much of a farmer and am certainly glad that I didn't farm for a living. Just before training camp, I had another idea on how to supply ourselves with steak before hockey games. Murray Oliver, Maniago, and a friend, Pete Karos, agreed to buy a couple of cows with me. I thought we could fatten up the animals, eventually have them butchered and have a good meat supply. It didn't work the way I had planned. I bought the cows in May, kept them in my pasture, and had the farmer come back in September to pick them up and quarter them. The farmer called and asked me, "What did you do to these cows?"

I told him, "Nothing, Why?"

He said, "You mustn't have fed them because they've lost 45 pounds!"

I thought they would gain the weight from grazing and from a salt block. I didn't know you had to feed them too. We wound up trading them in for some fat cattle, paid the difference and got our meat. I stayed away from the cattle business after that.

In addition to growing up in a great family environment, I have a wonderful family of my own. I have been fortunate to be with

Francine for most of my life. We have four tremendous children and 11 wonderful grandchildren.

I recall after the twins were born trying to get Mom and Dad to come to Minneapolis to see them and to help while Francine was in the hospital. I'm helpless around the house. They wouldn't come. They were working and could not take time off. I had heard it all before, plus they figured we would be home in the summer and they could see the kids then. I told them, "If you don't come here now and see the kids and help us out, we won't be coming home this summer and you won't see the grandkids."

When they arrived at our house the following day I know they had a good time and it helped me until Francine came home from the hospital.

I remember talking to my dad about my wedding some 48 years ago. The guest list was enormous and we were trying to cut it back some. It had reached 380 people. I told my dad maybe we didn't need to invite a certain relative as we never saw him. His words to me were straight and to the point. "Louie," he said, "You are talking about family. When you die, they will all be at your funeral and they are all coming to your wedding!" Dad understood what was most important —remember your family.

Mom, like Dad, was really quite the person. She was 63 years old when she died, so both my parents died at an early age. She was about 5'5" and weighed close to 200 pounds. It got plenty cold in the Soo but she never wore a coat in the winter. She would get up in the morning and walk a block to her clothing store without a coat. I don't know how she did it. Most of the time she even had on short sleeves.

She was not well near the end and struggled with diabetes. That didn't stop her. Once when she was having a big dish of ice cream, I said, "Mom, no ice cream. You keep eating that and you will lose a leg someday. You have to stop doing that."

"Louie," she said, "While I am here on this earth I am going to enjoy myself. I am eating this ice cream!"

When she died, I was so glad that I was able to make it to the hospital to see her. I had been at a Board of Governors meeting in Los Angeles and Francine and I had gone to Las Vegas for a short vacation following the meeting.

We had just arrived in Vegas and had walked into the MGM Grand Hotel as a phone call came from my sister. She said that Mom was real sick and they had taken her to a hospital in Sudbury. So we flew out right away through Toronto to Sudbury and got to the hospital just in time.

I still remember seeing her lying in the hospital bed and looking up at me. "Louie," she said, "It's so good to see you. How are you doing? Now Louie, I want you to remember something for me. I have had a good life. Your father is gone now and I don't want to be a burden on anyone, so if you try to keep me alive, I am going to kill you!" She did make it home for a short time before she died.

I have younger siblings, Michael and Julia, and the three of us have always been very close. My sister is the matriarch of the family, still lives in the Soo, and is the family organizer. She makes sure everything happens as it should and is relied upon by everyone in the family. She was an emergency room nurse, providing her expert skills to many patients. She also started a store with our cousin Janice—a basket shop using the same name as our mom's store, the Ideal Shoppe. My brother is a dentist and also is in the Soo. We all remain very close.

When my brother Michael finished dental school, he came to Minneapolis to pass his American boards. He needed a patient, so I volunteered. As the examination was going on, I thought I'd play a joke on him and the examiner by screaming out in pain. The examiner came running over to check on my condition, I had to quickly turn off the pain charade and tell the examiner I was his brother and just faking it. Neither of them thought it was very funny. In fact, I almost got him failed! I recall Michael saying to me, "Do that again, and I'll put this instrument right through your lip!"

I still see my brother and sister a few times a year. It is always a good time when we get together.

Once I had made the decision about college, I knew that professional hockey with the Blackhawks was probably not in the future for me. I was really positive about dental school and even though I made the switch later into business, my sights were set on a college education.

Michigan Tech was one of the first colleges to talk to me. They had a good hockey program, but for the most part it is an engineering school so I never really thought about going there. The next school was North Dakota. Eddie Tomlinson was from Sault Ste. Marie and he was playing there, so he told the coaches about me. Bob May was their hockey coach and he came to see us. He was giving us quite the pitch about the school and how I could play hockey there and how wonderful it would be for me.

Mom and Dad sat there listening to Bob while Eddie had me off to the side telling how great it was at North Dakota and how much fun I would have as a student.

The recruiting visit took a sour note when Coach May asked me what I wanted to study in school. I told him dentistry. He said, "Well, that's good, you can go your four years at North Dakota and *then* you can go to dental school." It definitely was not in my plan to go to college for four years and then go to dental school. To me, that sounded like a waste of time. Then he tried to talk me into business school. It didn't work, and soon North Dakota was out of the picture. Ironically enough, one year later I was in business school at the U, and Bob May quit coaching and came to Minnesota's dental school. May was the one who told John Mariucci about me and while I was trying to decide what to do, Mariucci called me and asked if I would visit the University of Minnesota.

I had never heard of him or the University of Minnesota. He said he wanted me to fly to Minneapolis and visit the campus. I agreed, even though I had to ask my parents where Minneapolis was.

When I made the trip to the Twin Cities, they put me up at the Nicollet Hotel in Minneapolis. It was really warm out, and the hotel had no air conditioning, so I put cold water in the tub and slept there. Besides my tour of the campus and getting to know John Mariucci, I spent a lot of my time in Minneapolis at the movies. During the short time I was there, I went to nine movies, three a night as I recall, and on one of the nights in between I went to a fraternity rush party.

Immediately, I felt the University of Minnesota was the right place for me, so I signed up with the U before I returned home.

I started at the University of Minnesota in the fall of 1960. Dad and my uncle drove me down to school, and stayed just long enough to get me situated in Frontier Hall. I can still picture them driving away and leaving me there. I had never felt so alone. I didn't know anyone, and there I was just standing there.

I got settled into Frontier Hall and met my roommate, Louie Karakas, a goalie from Eveleth, Minnesota. I was all set to go to school, play hockey, and become a dentist. I had no worries about the education part of it. I was always a good student and worked very hard to get good grades. As far as the hockey part went, I had plenty of confidence.

Although I was somewhat of a "cut up" in school, Mom always made sure I got my homework done before I went anywhere and that I kept up my grades. But even with that, I still had some fun in school and was somewhat of a wiseguy in class. I was just having some fun for the most part, but did acquire somewhat of a reputation.

I remember one teacher who asked on the first day of class, "Is there a Lou Nanne in here?" When I answered, I was told that I had a reserved seat right in the front row.

Playing hockey at Minnesota was a change for me. There was a rule that you could not body-check anyone over the red line. That was different from the hockey I played in Canada, where we could hit someone anywhere on the ice. It took me some time to adjust to this style because in Canada that contact was a big part of the game. Also for the first time, I had to get used to wearing a helmet, which I had never worn before. (I guess that explains the stitches.)

Freshmen were not eligible to play with the varsity during those days, but Mariucci had me practicing with the varsity squad. I was the only freshmen player who practiced all week with the varsity and then played games on the weekends with the freshmen.

Once I started playing varsity hockey, I found I had some stiff competition. The University of Denver was probably the best team in the league, but we didn't play against them because our two coaches didn't get along. Mariucci didn't like Murray Armstrong. John hated the fact that Denver recruited older Canadian players. He thought they should come down when they were 18 years old, not after they had finished Junior A hockey.

When we played Denver in the NCAA tournament he had me carry a sign off the plane that read, "We are going to fry Canadian bacon." At the banquet, John introduced our team by saying we had 19 future presidents and one prime minister. Unfortunately, when we met them in the semifinals, they dominated us 6–1.

Even though most of my hockey-playing friends were playing junior hockey in Canada, I was happy at school. I was the first one that I know of who left to attend college so it was quite different for me than with most kids from the Soo.

Every summer during school, I would come home and go to work in the steel plant, and my connections at home have always remained very strong. This also enabled me to have spending money while I was at college and lessen the burden on my parents.

My days of playing hockey in the streets in front of our house had moved onto a bigger stage. I was well on my way from the Soo to the U.

2

John Mariucci

His name was John Mariucci. He was the head hockey coach at the University of Minnesota and he was an imposing guy. Along with my father and Walter Bush, he had the most influence on me of anyone on my life. We hit it off the very first time we met. I don't know exactly why. It was a wonderful relationship that lasted close to 30 years.

You would never know it by the unmerciful manner in which he treated me on the ice, but from the time I arrived at the University of Minnesota from Sault Ste. Marie, Ontario, John took me under his wing and truly watched out for me and my family. He was a great person.

John Mariucci was born in Eveleth, Minnesota, and played hockey and football at the University of Minnesota. He was an exceptional athlete and although he had some National Football League teams interested in him, he was an All-American hockey player at Minnesota and stayed with hockey. He played for five years with the Chicago Blackhawks and was known for his fierce play and physical toughness.

John had a great playing career, a solid coaching career at the University of Minnesota, and did a fantastic job as the assistant general manager of the Minnesota North Stars for 20 years. But more than ever he was known for his relentless efforts to assist the American-born hockey player. He is most appropriately recognized as the "Godfather of American Hockey."

When he coached the Gophers, he was noted for his recruitment of Minnesota players. Because of his incredible passion and his constant promotion of American players, high school hockey in Minnesota spread faster than in any other state in the U.S. Between 1952 and 1980 a handful of teams grew to more than 150.

Since 1983 the John Mariucci Award has been given to the high school hockey coach of the year, as selected by the high school coaches. The award in honor of John represents his work with Minnesota players and coaches; he is certainly one of the most notable of all Minnesota sports figures and personalities. In fact, he did more for American hockey than anyone I have known, and I have such high regard and respect for him for the remarkable commitment that he made in his life. I know John would have gone to any length to make absolutely sure that every American hockey player was treated fairly and equally. And if they were good enough, he wanted them to have the opportunity to play.

John Mariucci was one of the few American players in the National Hockey League during his era. He saw this as an opportunity to give American players the same chance. He worked his entire life toward that objective. Needless to say, he was successful.

I first talked to John Mariucci in 1959, when he recruited me to come to the University of Minnesota. I met him when I arrived in Minneapolis and later asked my dad, "How old is this guy?" Dad said, "Well, he can't be that old. I think he retired from the Blackhawks about 15 years ago." I thought he looked about 65. And of course I had no idea at the time of the impact this man would have on me for the rest of my life.

There is no doubt that he kept me in the game after my years with the U.S. Olympic Team, which resulted in me signing a professional hockey contract with the Minnesota North Stars and was the main force behind my becoming a Minnesota resident for life. I recall John telling me when he recruited me that if I decided to come to Minnesota, I would never leave. He was certainly prophetic in his pronouncement because I have lived here ever since.

John did everything for me. I was engaged to be married as a junior at the university and got married during the summer of my senior year. John was the sponsor for my wife to come to the United States and work, which enabled her to get her visa. He got her a job and made sure we were doing all right. Many times John would go to Francine before the games and tease her, "Now Francine, if Lou doesn't play well tonight, you go back to the Soo without him."

We just connected as player and coach and personally. He saw something in me that was very much like him. I was an Italian kid, he was an Italian kid. He knew I was here from Canada and didn't know anyone, so he looked out for me. John gave me his No. 2 to wear for the Gophers. He was a defenseman as I was. It really meant a lot to me that he did that.

Even though he usually appeared to be a gruff and tough character, John was a deeply caring and sensitive man. He was considerate of others and a remarkable human being. He always went out of his way to take care of his players and make sure they were always doing the right thing.

I think another reason John and I got along so well was that he liked the fact that I took my education seriously. It was very important to John that his players did well in their classes. We always appreciated that about him and even though he was as hard-nosed as they come, everyone liked him and enjoyed playing hockey for him.

I definitely took my own studies seriously—and I took a lot of pride in my success. I remember one of the Minnesota Gophers football players on the great teams of the 1960s was Julian Hook, a terrific linebacker. I took a history class from Professor Beatty with Julian. At the end of class one day, Professor Beatty told us that he would make a sample test available for students to review before the upcoming midquarter exam. He said it would give us an idea of the types of questions that would be on the test. All we had to do was come to his office and pick up a sample copy.

Later on that day Hook and I went to Professor Beatty's office to pick up our sample. When we got there, the professor was not around so we asked his teaching assistant for the sample test. We then took the test back to my apartment and spent most of the evening studying. We went over all the questions and felt that we were well prepared for the exam.

The next day we went to class to take the real test. The professor said to the class, "Now, I want you to pay attention to what I am going to say. There will be no noise in the class and no questions. I don't want anyone raising their hand and asking a question. Finish your test, bring it up to my desk and leave. Okay, I'm going to hand out the papers now, so no talking and no questions."

As soon as I received my test paper, I knew there was a problem. Julian looked over at me and knew the same thing. I put up my hand. "Mr. Nanne, I told you there would not be any questions. Now put your hand down," he admonished.

I said, "But sir, I have to talk to you."

"Mr. Nanne," he said, "Put your hand down and do the test."

So we took the test, walked up and handed it to him. The professor stopped us and said, "Okay, now what was the issue you had?"

I told him that we had come to his office yesterday, as he had suggested, and picked up the sample tests. The problem was we didn't get the sample test from the teaching assistant, we got the real test. "That's why I had my hand up to tell you what had happened. If you would like us to take a different test or a verbal test, just let us know."

Professor Beatty looked at us and said, "You two guys are gentlemen and scholars and honest young men. I am not going to do anything about this and I am going to let your tests stand as is." The next day he contacted the *Minnesota Daily* newspaper and told them the story. Obviously we were graded as he said and we each received an A.

When I graduated, Mariucci made me his assistant coach. He told me that if I was not going to turn professional at the time, he wanted me to coach the freshman team. Initially I told him that I would not be able to do it because I had a job and worked during the day. The freshmen practiced from 2:00 PM to 4:30 PM every afternoon during the season, which wouldn't work for me. That wasn't an issue as John changed the practice hours to accommodate my schedule. He wanted me to stay with him at the university. John was always there for me, looking out for me and guiding me to make the right decisions.

He was constantly prodding me to do things that he knew would be right for me. He was like a father to me. Dad was way off in the Soo but John was in Minnesota and he filled the role admirably.

When I first came to Minnesota on a recruiting visit, John picked me up and asked me what I wanted to do to get acquainted with the university. I told him that I wanted to visit the dental school because I was going to be a dentist. He looked at me and said, "You are supposed to be knocking people's teeth out, not putting them in!"

As he took me around the city and campus on my visit everything was new to me. I didn't even know where Minneapolis was! I had to go to my mom and ask her. She told me it was somewhere near a town named Rochester, because that was where the Mayo Clinic was located, and we had a relative who had gone there.

When I arrived in Minneapolis and before John picked me up, I had been talking to a taxi driver about Minnesota in general, the weather here and so forth. I don't mind the cold too much, but I don't like snow. In fact, I absolutely hate snow.

The driver told me I had nothing to worry about. "We have cold winters here in Minnesota," he said, "but only an average of about three inches of snow for the winter." That was fine with me. I could handle the three inches just fine. No problem. When I went home and told my dad I was going to come to the University of Minnesota to play hockey and go to dental school, at first he balked at the idea. I said, "Dad, they only get three inches of snow there for the whole winter. I'm going!"

John drove me around the campus and to the dental school and then took me to a lunch meeting. He was selling for a paper company in addition to his coaching, and had a meeting with a client at a restaurant called McCarthy's out on Highway 12. At this time in my life, I truly did not know anything about anything. I mean nothing! Going to a fancy restaurant with the head hockey coach at the University of Minnesota for a business luncheon was way out of my league. But I went along, having little choice in the matter.

We sat down at our table and the waitress came over and asked me what I wanted to drink so I said, "I'll have a beer." I guess I thought that was the right thing to do. I thought, here we are out to lunch at a bar and I'm asked at this business meeting what I wanted to drink. I thought a beer was the appropriate thing to order. No one said anything. About a year or so later, John says to me one day, "By the way, what the hell were you thinking about that day when I took you to that bar/restaurant on your recruiting visit and you ordered a beer? Here you are underage getting recruited at the time and you are ordering beer to drink." I said to him, "John, what were you thinking? Here I am underage and you bring me into a bar on my recruiting visit? The waitress came over and asked me what I wanted to drink. I didn't know anything. It was all new to me so I just ordered a beer. What was I supposed to do? I don't even drink but I thought that's what you expected me to do." We had a laugh about that.

I loved playing hockey at Minnesota and I loved playing for Coach Mariucci. He was as tough as they come. I know for a fact that if he was in a fight and getting physically beaten, he would never stop coming at you; he would never, ever give up. He'd say only God was his master and he would never let someone get the best of him. He knew it and everyone who ever knew him knew it too.

John was so much fun to tease, especially when he didn't know that we were joking with him. We certainly put him on after we had just won the RPI Tournament out East and were taking a bus back to New York City to catch our flight to Minneapolis. We knew that John believed that no one could hold a candle to his toughness. Ron Constantine—my roommate from John's hometown, Eveleth—and I cooked up a plan to aggravate him.

We knew that the night we returned to town there was a St. Paul "Fighting" Saints game. We also knew that the Saints had a guy playing for them by the name of John Bailey. Bailey was a real tough guy, a noted fighter who wasn't afraid to take someone apart with his stick. When I was the stick boy for the Sault Ste. Marie Greyhounds, I got to know John because he played for the team. He had a terrific slap shot that he was known for, but he was more recognized for his fighting and was willing to go after anyone, stick included.

In addition, the Saints were playing the Minneapolis Millers in that game. It was going to be a classic battle. The Millers had a player and enforcer named Cy Whiteside, and whenever the two teams met,

Bailey and Whiteside were likely to go after each other. They were involved in some incredible brawls.

On the bus back to New York City, "Tino"—Ron Constantine—and I were sitting on the bus right in back of Mariucci. I said really loud so John could hear, "Tino, when we get back in town we should go see the Saints play the Millers. Those Saints, they got some real tough guys on their team." Tino caught on right away what I was up to. I said, "Those Saints are mean and they got this John Bailey who is the toughest guy I ever saw. I know for a fact that there is no player in hockey that is tougher than John Bailey!"

So then Tino jumps in and says, "Yeah, he sure is. I wouldn't even dress or get on the ice with Bailey. He is scary." Then I said, "Boy you're right, Tino. Can you even imagine playing against a guy like that? I would never want to do that." And we kept it up and kept it up knowing that John was listening to everything we were saying.

Finally, John just blew up. With fire in his face he turned around in his seat and said to us, "You ———, you think Bailey is so tough, you don't know anything! He is nothing but a piece of cake. I'll show you two who is tough. You don't know what you are talking about. I'm going to call Ken Yackel (coach of the Millers) and suit up the next game for the Millers. And I will guarantee you that John Bailey won't come out of the locker room for the second period!"

I told him, "John, don't do that. You are too old to play again. You will get hurt. He might kill you. Don't do it. Don't talk like that! You are afraid to sit at the top of a Ferris wheel. You're afraid of heights, John. Don't do it. We need you to be our coach. You'll get killed, John!"

Mariucci was absolutely fuming. He hollered at us and said, "Listen you dumb ———, I'll show you." And we got into this huge argument. It was unbelievable. We really put him on. It was beautiful.

John just could not allow anyone to actually think that someone else was tougher than him. He could not contain himself.

We had so much fun baiting him because his reaction was just what we expected. So the more mad he got and the more he reacted, the more we laid it on him. But the bottom line of the whole charade was that if John did call Yackel and showed up for the game, John Bailey likely would not have come out for the second period! We loved John and just delighted in his reactions.

I always felt that I could go to John for anything. He was the type of person who was willing to help you in any way possible. He was constantly going to bat for USA Hockey and all of the colleges, trying to get American kids the opportunity play professionally.

John would spend 75 to 100 nights a year going around the state talking to get kids to get them interested in hockey and building rinks for youth hockey. He did everything he possibly could do to improve and accentuate interest in hockey in the state of Minnesota. And there was no question about his success at doing what he loved to do.

John Mariucci is legendary in Minnesota hockey lore. He never stopped in his pursuit to support the American player; his passion never wavered. There were no restrictions on his time and no measures that he wouldn't go to in order to assist American players to succeed. He just simply was driven by the underlying motive to provide the opportunity to players in the United States. He was like an evangelist going around the state preaching his messages about Minnesota hockey.

The absolute best tribute ever to this man was to have the University of Minnesota hockey arena named after him. Initially the university changed the hockey side of Williams Arena to honor John, and then in 1993, when the U built a new hockey arena on campus, they named it Mariucci Arena. I cannot think of any other person anywhere who is more deserving.

In the hockey communities all over the state, John was well respected and people enjoyed being around him. When I was playing for the Gophers, we used to take the train to Michigan when we had our weekend series with Michigan and Michigan State. On the way back we would stop in Chicago. On Sunday nights, when the Blackhawks were playing at home, he would take us to the game. I can remember times that we would be in the elevator at the stadium with John and players and coaches for the NHL teams would get on the elevator with us. When they saw John their reaction was incredible. They loved him and just enjoyed seeing him again. One night I witnessed the special relationship he had with the legendary Montreal Canadiens coach, Toe Blake. You could feel electricity in the air, the warmth of their smiles, and the love when they hugged one another. John used to terrorize the Canadiens when he played in the NHL, but in the elevator it was pure respect.

I will say, however, that when John got mad, he could really get mad! One night we were in Michigan playing his close friend Amo Bessone's Michigan State Spartans team. I can't even remember the score of the game but I will never forget what occurred afterward.

Most of the players that night had disregarded the team rules and spent most of the night out having a good time. We were scheduled to leave on the train at 2:00 AM for Chicago, a four-hour trip. When we arrived there, we would get hotel rooms and go to the game the following night.

Some of the players were quite loud when they got on the train. Others had a difficult time hiding their behavior, but the worst of it all was using John Mariucci's bathroom before he arrived. Most of the team was too rowdy to sleep so we all looked forward to the hotel room where we could get some rest. Mariucci said nothing at the time.

When we arrived in Chicago, John told us to grab our suitcases and hockey equipment bags. As some started to walk to the taxi stand for the ride to the hotel, John stopped us. "No, no" he told us. "We are walking to the hotel." And we did, eight blocks from the train station to the LaSalle Hotel with our suitcases and hockey bags at 6:00 in the morning. It was brutal.

When we got to the hotel, John went to the front desk and said to the clerk, "Minnesota Gophers." "Yes sir, we have your rooms for you, Mr. Mariucci," he was told by the clerk. John responded by saying, "No, we will only need three rooms this trip. One room will be for me, one for our trainer, and the third room will be for the team." He looked over to us and said, "You want to fly with the owls during the night, you can fly with the eagles during the day." And they jammed us all in one room.

Some of us found a movie theater open early that morning and went there to sleep. Another one of our players taped himself to the wall to try to sleep standing up. John got his message across to the team very clearly on that particular trip.

When I arrived at the university from Sault Ste. Marie freshmen were not eligible at the time, though John had me practicing with the varsity. We had solid teams while I was there and we all worked very hard. John was really tough on us and for some reason he picked on me especially in practice and in the games. He never let up. He later told me that he used me as an example because he knew that I could take it. It was odd to me, because we always had this great relationship, but on the ice, he was very rough on me.

John was always on the ice during practice and really showed me how to play defense. He was a great teacher. He knew the game very well and taught me all of the ins and outs of the game. He showed me how to use the nets to my advantage, how to use the boards, and how to stand up and meet the play as it came toward me. I learned a lot from him but still took quite a shellacking from him in practice and during the games.

I recall one night we were playing the United States National Team up in Virginia, Minnesota. It was my first game and we could not find a way to put the puck in the net. Tommy Yurkovich, the Nationals goalie, was stopping everything that we shot at him.

In the second period, they were leading us 1–0. I came to the bench and saw one of our players fire a high shot at the net. Yurkovich went after it and the puck hit his glove and bounced off onto the ice. When I saw him fail in his attempt to catch the puck, I hollered at the guys, "Keep shooting at this guy, he can't catch!"

I was just talking on the bench, trying to get the guys going. Mariucci was standing near me and heard what I was saying. So John turned to me and said, "Are you saying this guy can't catch the puck? Are you telling the guys to shoot high at him because he can't catch the high shots?" I said, "No, no, John, I'm just saying to shoot at him, just shoot at him." So he fires back at me, "Well, I'm telling everyone to shoot low on the net. You don't tell them to shoot high!" I said again, "John, I didn't tell them to shoot high, I just told them to shoot." Then he was really mad. He hollered at me, "Well, shut up!"

The second period came to an end and we were still behind 1–0. In the locker room as we are getting ready to go back on the ice for the third period, Mariucci looks at me and says, "And you, Nanne, don't you ever tell the guys to shoot high at Yurkovich again!" I was really frustrated now so I said it again, "John, I did not say to shoot high." "Yes you did," he shouted at me. I came back at him with, "No I didn't tell them that. I just told the guys to shoot at him." Mariucci says, "Well, don't tell them to shoot high again." I followed with, "I didn't!" "Yes you did," he shouted and it kept going back and forth. It was unbelievable.

Finally, John said, "That's it, Nanne, take your uniform off! You are not playing!" Now I got really upset. I had an orange in my hand

and I just turned and threw it in disgust. It actually came close to hitting John as it bounced off the wall.

So there I was sitting in the locker room and the team was out on the ice for the third period and we're behind 1–0. Pretty soon I hear the score is 2–0 so I ask our trainer to ask John if I can play. He comes back and tells me, "John said no!" Then the score was 3–0. I get another "No!" At 4–0 I asked our trainer to ask John again and I got another "No!" At 5–0, another "No!"

The team came into the locker room and John didn't say a word. He came over and threw me his car keys. John let me take his car home so I could spend time with my family in the Soo during our school break. After all that had happened, he still gave me his car keys. It was the way he was.

Everyone on the team figured I wouldn't come back after the school break, that I would leave the team for good and play junior hockey in Canada. But that didn't happen. I came back and everything was fine.

The absolute worst fight between us happened while we were playing in North Dakota. It was my junior year, and we had to win one of the two games to get in the playoffs. John had told me before the third period to stay out of the penalty box. I had just taken a penalty and got out without them scoring on us. We were tied at the end of the second period and he said to me, "Nanne, if you throw one punch, you will never play here again."

So of course I wound up getting thrown out of the game for fighting. And in college hockey if you get in a fight and get tossed, it means you cannot play the second game of the series. It was a bad scene. And to make matters worse, the vice president of the university was in the stands watching us play. As a Sioux forward tried to stick handle past me, I hit him and he retaliated with his stick. I grabbed him and wrestled him to the ice, remembering what John had told me about throwing a punch or fighting.

While I am struggling with the Sioux player, I can hear Mariucci screaming at me from the bench, "Throw a punch, Nanne, and you are done here for good!" I didn't. I made sure that I did not throw any punches.

So now the two of us are sent to the penalty box for roughing. No punches were thrown. We were just jawing at each other, and after a stoppage in play he jumped on my back and the fight began. Mariucci sent my roommate, Ron Constantine, over to the penalty box to tell me I better not throw another punch or he and I would both be finished. Before he could bring me John's message the fight was in full bloom, and Ron realized the message would be for naught.

Tino came into the box and said, "Keep punching, Lou, you are done here anyway!" Because the fight didn't stop, John came across the ice to assist in breaking it up. We lost 3–2 and I was ineligible for the next night as well.

We lost the second game of the North Dakota series 4–0 and missed the playoffs. John threw me off the team and said I would never play again for the university, and so that put me in a very tough position. Here I was too old to play junior hockey in Canada, I would lose my scholarship, and wouldn't have the money to continue school. I couldn't imagine what the future would be like.

I was engaged to be married and all these things were racing through my head. I didn't know what my future was going to be.

I was really upset when Mariucci came into the locker room after the game. I challenged John to a fight. We went at it. And at just about the point when he was ready to take a swing at me and probably put me in the hospital, he suddenly put his hands in his pockets and walked out of the room. I went after John down the hallway and hollered at him, "Get back in here!" He continued to walk away and said to me, "You will never play here again!" I was devastated.

And on top of all this we lost the game and then lost again the next night while I pondered my future. It certainly didn't appear I had any future at the University of Minnesota.

On the train coming back to Minneapolis and about every 50 miles or so I asked the trainer to go and ask John if I can play again. Our final game was on Monday night, an exhibition game against the Swedish national team. The answer always came back the same. "No! No! No! No!" Soon after we arrived at the station and just as we were getting off the train, our trainer came to me and said, "John says you can play again." It was an unbelievable few days but I was back as a Minnesota Gopher hockey player.

There was no doubt I was John's whipping boy but I still had such tremendously strong feelings for the man. He was very special to me. Once the game or practice was over, he was always there for me. "What do you need? What can I do for you? Is everything okay? How is the studying going?" That was John, like a second father to me.

I got married that summer and things were going really well for me. My grades were good and I expected to have a tremendous senior year playing hockey at Minnesota. And there for me, always concerned about my needs, was John Mariucci.

He would often come to me before the games and ask if I needed any tickets. I would take whatever I could get and sell them. Things were different then than they are now. During the NCAA playoffs in Denver, I had some friends and friends of my friends who wanted tickets. I left them in their names at the box office and asked them to bring me the money at our bench.

As we were warming up before the game, I would take a shot, go to the bench, get my money, take a shot, go to the bench, and get my money. I stuffed the money in my gloves and took it to the locker room when we were through. John helped me make a few extra dollars to pay for my expenses by allowing me to have extra tickets.

During my junior year, I was scheduling my classes and I needed a one-credit elective course. John was teaching a class on "hockey coaching," a one-credit class in the undergraduate school. So I took his class thinking it would be a piece of cake.

After the first class, John asks me to come and see him. He says to me, "What are you doing here taking my class?" I told him that I needed the credit so I decided to take it. He told me, "Look, if you think I am going to fight with you every day in practice and then have to come and fight with you in class, I'm not going to do it. If you stay away from class and never show up again, I'll give you an A. Show up here again, you get a D." I never showed up again and got an A.

John was an exceptional coach. He knew the fundamentals and his game plan was basically pressure hockey. He took pride in his teams getting all over their opponents all of the time. He wasn't much of a between-periods or before-the-game *rah rah* guy. He was very direct and to the point, always straightforward with us and he wouldn't accept anything but total effort. He knew we couldn't win on talent alone.

We always carried six defensemen on the team. One night we were playing in Michigan against the Wolverines and things weren't going so well for us. Michigan was really putting it to us and John was furious. So my defensive partner and I took our shift on the ice and had a difficult time controlling their pressure on us. When we came back to the bench, John yelled at us, "Back row!"

Whenever John had it in his mind that he was going to bench someone for poor play, he would yell, "Back row." That meant you had to go and sit in the back row of the bench and you knew you wouldn't be going back out.

So now the next set of defensemen come off of their shift on the ice and Mariucci yells at them, "Back row!" The third set of defensemen finished their shift doing just as poorly and John hollers at them,

"Back row." Now all six defensemen are sitting in the back row and there is no one to go out on the ice to play defense. John starts screaming, "Where in the hell are all of our defensemen?" I yell back, "We are all in the back row!" John turned to us and bellowed, "Get your —— back on the ice!" He was a classic!

One night we played in North Dakota when it was bitterly cold outside and just about as bad in the arena. The North Dakota arena was as cold as it got. I used to wear leather gloves under my hockey gloves to keep my hands warm. My cousin, who played hockey for Michigan Tech, used to take a sock, cut slots for two eyes, a nose, and a mouth and wear the whole sock over his head to keep warm when they played there. It was just brutally cold there, by far the worst arena in the league.

The game was really close and both teams were playing extremely well. It seemed like we were going back and forth up the ice equally all night long. Bill Ramsey, our left-winger, went offside when we had a 3-on-2 rush, and Mariucci blew his stack. He started screaming at Ramsey as he came off the ice. Ramsey had to go right by John to get to the bench because John was standing at the door. Now Ramsey was hot under the collar, too, and as he entered the bench area, he took out his anger on the door by slamming it shut. John looked over toward Ramsey and shouted at him, "Open the —— door!" Ramsey shot back, "Why? I just closed it!" "Because my hand is in it," shrieked Mariucci. It was just one of those nights.

I do honestly think the most upset that I ever saw John happened in a game against Michigan State in East Lansing. John's close friend Amo Bessone was the coach of the Spartans and John always had the highest respect for him as a person and as a hockey coach. They always partied at each other's homes after each game.

Bessone spent 28 years as the head hockey coach at Michigan State and won the NCAA hockey championship in 1966. He coached

Michigan State for 814 games during his tenure and was instrumental in coaching 12 All-Americans in leading the Spartans to three Big Ten titles and a tie for another.

During the game, my roommate Ron Constantine got into a skirmish on the ice. Both players were careful not to get into an actual fight because they would be suspended. The referee called Tino for a roughing penalty, and on the way to the penalty box he skated over to the Michigan State bench and started yelling at Bessone, John's closest friend in hockey. So now on top of the two-minute roughing penalty, he got a 10-minute misconduct penalty. John went absolutely nuts! He was so mad at Tino for his behavior that he told him afterward, "You're done! I'm sending you home!"

The team had made arrangements for Constantine to fly home in the morning. After the game I asked to see John at the hotel. That was my senior year, and Constantine was my roommate. So I went to Mariucci's room and said to him, "John, you can't do this to the kid. You know him. You know his family. You have known him his whole life. Don't do this. Let him play. We are almost finished with the regular season and we have playoffs next week."

John was still really upset. He said to me, "I'm not going to put up with that. He had no business going over there and arguing with Bessone. He can't act like that out there. He is never going to play here again. He's going home!" I said, "Yes, yes, I agree with you. He was wrong to do that, but John, please don't do this. You will destroy this kid. Give him another chance. We need him."

Finally I brought John around to my way of thinking and he said, "Okay, okay, go tell him he can play." I was so relieved when he changed his mind. I thought there was no chance he would ever let Tino play again after what he did.

So the next night during the game Constantine got into another skirmish on the ice and believe it or not went after Bessone again at the Michigan State bench. John benched him for the rest of the game and he never played again for the Gophers.

Even though John took me to task a lot during my years with the team, he still found a way to look out for me—even when I didn't deserve it. During my first year at Minnesota freshmen were not eligible to play on the varsity, but John let me travel with the team to North Dakota.

North Dakota had recruited me quite heavily and John knew it. When he asked me to go with the varsity on the weekend trip to Grand Forks he told me, "I want to show you how lucky you are to be going to Minnesota."

One of my friends, Eddie Tomlinson, was playing for the Sioux, so after the game, I met up with Eddie and some of his buddies and we went out on the town. Now there is not a lot to do nightlifewise in Grand Forks but we had a great time. So the following year when I was eligible, after our first game I hooked up with some of the guys from North Dakota and they invited me to a fraternity party. I went with our goalie, Charlie Steinwick, who was my roommate.

We had a great time at the party and dragged ourselves in about 4:00 AM. Because it was way past curfew, we carefully attempted to get to our rooms without being seen. Our trainer caught us coming in the back door of the hotel and told Mariucci. John was upset and told Steinwick he was not playing but he left me alone. All he ever told me was, "Don't do it again or I'll sit you too!"

I felt kind of guilty because he punished my roommate. Now that I think about it, maybe John was catching up with me during the next three years when he made me his whipping boy at practice, during games, and every time we hit the ice. If John was still with us, I would ask him about that.

He would come up with sayings that everyone copied. One of his best happened to my teammate, Rick Alm. John came in at the end of a period against Colorado College and yelled at everyone. On his way out he looked and saw Rick next to me. He walked out, remembered he missed Rick, and walked back in and said his classic remark. "Rick, you get worse and worse every day, and today you're playing like next month."

John cared deeply about people and about the University of Minnesota. Having played both hockey and football at the university, it meant a lot to John to be the head hockey coach. It was very important to him that each of his players represented the university very well and he would not put up with anything less than total effort.

As players, he was always more than just tough on us, sometimes he was brutally tough, but we had such great respect for John that it was an honor to play for him. He made sure that we graduated on time in four years and we had many respectable professions that players entered into for their careers.

After leaving the University of Minnesota, John became the assistant general manager of the Minnesota North Stars and stayed in that position until his death in 1987. When I became the general manager we were working closely together again trying to rebuild the team. He was my right-hand guy and I truly loved being around him.

One day John's wife, Gretchen, called me and said, "Lou, John is never going to tell you anything about this, but he is in a lot of pain every day. He has a real bad back and he won't go to the doctor." She told me that it had been going on for several months with him. I told her not to worry about it and that I would take care of it right away.

I went to John in the office and said, "John, what are you doing this weekend?" He said, "I'm going out to Michigan to see Michigan and Michigan State play. There are some college kids in the series that I want to take a look at." I told him, "Look, you are not going anywhere. I am told that you have a bad back." He says to me, "No, it's okay." I said, "No, it's not okay and you are going to do something about it right now." I told him that Gretchen had called me and told me and that she was really worried about his health.

John was upset now and told me, "I'm not going to any doctor. I'm just fine!" Then he got me upset and I said to him, "John, you are not traveling anymore until you go and see a doctor. You can sit right here in this office but you are not going anywhere until you get this taken care of right now!"

I finally got him to see a doctor and they found that he had prostate cancer in the advanced stages. If he had just not been so stubborn and gone in earlier, they might have been able to do something for him. But it was too late.

He suffered a great deal the last few months of his life. In many respects John likely saved my life. After John's death, I paid more attention to my health and went to the Mayo Clinic for regular check-ups. Because of this, they caught my prostate cancer early and it saved me. You could say I owe my health to John.

Herb Brooks and I were pallbearers at John's funeral. I told Herbie, "I've wanted you to coach the North Stars for the past nine years and John wanted you there as well. It's time to do it." Herbie looked at me and said, "I think you're right." John helped me to finally make it happen.

So he was gone. I had spent almost three decades with him and learned so much from him. His passion, strong beliefs in providing inspiration and opportunities for the American player, and his leadership at the University of Minnesota and with the North Stars will live on in my heart forever. He gave so much and asked so little of others. He only asked for you to give your best and be a person of honesty and integrity. He was easy to follow in that mold. He provided me with guidance and became a second father to me. Thank you, John. I miss you.

3

The U.S. Olympic Team

We shouldn't have been there at all. In fact, we were
breaking team rules. It was pitch black outside. I went over
the fence first and landed in muddy water past my ankles.
Herbie, on the other side of the fence, asked me how it went.
"Everything is just fine," I told him. "Come on over." He
made quite the sight as he splashed to a muddy landing. It
became an indelible Olympic memory for both of us.

When I graduated from the University of Minnesota I felt I would have an opportunity to play professional hockey. I had made the Western Collegiate Hockey Association All-Star Team in 1963, and also won the WCHA Most Valuable Player Award the same year. I was an NCAA West first-team All-American and the first defenseman ever to lead the WCHA in scoring. My three years—1961 to 1963—playing for John Mariucci and the Minnesota Gophers were phenomenal. I have so many wonderful memories playing hockey and attending the university. Those four years of school went by in a flash.

After finishing my college eligibility, I joined the United States Hockey League in 1962, playing for the Rochester Mustangs. In 1967, Murray Williamson and Walter Bush were helping to put together the U.S. Olympic Hockey Team that would play in Grenoble, France, in 1968. The two men were instrumental in convincing me to play. They always believed I would be a good Olympian. The only problem was, I was Canadian. They asked me if I was willing to transfer my citizenship. In 1967 a bill went through Congress and I received instant citizenship. I became an American and an Olympic hockey player.

I had wanted to play professional hockey but I was set in my ways. I felt that I had to have the absolute right kind of contract—otherwise, I had no intention of playing. I am very glad that I did not turn professional earlier. Otherwise, I never would have had that Olympic year.

When I was growing up in Sault Ste. Marie I never gave any thought about Olympic hockey or playing in the Olympics. But then when I came to the United Sates and attended the University of Minnesota, I got more familiar with what it was all about. I was on the hockey team at Minnesota when the 1960 Olympic Team won the gold medal. Today they call that the "forgotten miracle." Well, I remember it quite well. It was amazing.

The Olympic hero that year was the great Jack McCartan, the U.S. goalie. He was tremendous. The fact that he was from Minnesota made my initial connection to Olympic hockey even greater. He was certainly one of the most well known and decorated of the players and it seemed as though he stopped every shot taken at his goal.

After the Olympics, Jack signed professionally to play for the New York Rangers. At the time, he was one of few Americans in the league at all. He played in four games during the 1959–60 season, and then only eight more in the following year. After the 1960–61 season, he never played in the NHL again. Jack continued professionally and played minor league hockey up until the early 1970s and then played for three years with the Minnesota Fighting Saints of the WHA. He later became a scout for the Vancouver Canucks.

When I was at the U, the 1960 team played and practiced at Williams Arena, so I had a firsthand look at that squad. I had the opportunity to play against Jack McCartan when I was playing for the Gophers and we scrimmaged the Olympic team. The immensity of the players' responsibility was definitely impressed upon me. The goal to play in the Olympics grew in me as I began to understand its significance.

There have been ice hockey tournaments at the Olympic Games since 1920, so the history is estimable. In the beginning, men's games were introduced in the Summer Olympics. Then when the Winter Olympics were introduced in 1924, hockey became a part of the winter games. Until 1998, Olympic hockey was strictly for amateur players.

There is no question that once the Olympic competition turned professional, it changed the entire scope of the Games. In many ways, it forced the game to take on a whole new look. The "Miracle on Ice"—the Americans' famous upset of the Soviet hockey team in 1980—would never have had the impact it did if professional players had been on the U.S. team.

I have always preferred Olympic hockey with amateur players, though it is much better hockey with professionals. Still, employing professionals just seems to take some of the spirit of it all away. Before the switch, the system gave young kids an opportunity to have a life-changing experience. It gave them the goal of making the Olympic Team and winning for their country. I always felt that it was an important aspect of Olympic competition and that it created those David versus Goliath games. That part is now missing.

The real reason that professionals were introduced into the games originated with skiers. Many of them started to get big contracts in advertising and would not participate in the Olympics otherwise. The IOC didn't want to lose those athletes because it was a big event in the Winter Olympics, so they changed the rules. In doing so, I believe that they took away some of the romance of the Games.

I equate it to the Minnesota high school tournament games in basketball and hockey. Nowadays there are multiple divisions and classes of play. Basketball seems to have undergone the most change. Now, with so many brackets, I don't think they'll ever have a tournament upset as incredible as the Edgerton High School championship win in 1960. I still remember that little school finishing the regular season undefeated, then coming to the Twin Cities and beating perennial powerhouse Austin for the state championship. I believe Edgerton had something like 60 students in their whole school—and they came to the Cities and won it all. It was magnificent!

In the first three decades of Olympic hockey, Canada dominated, winning six of seven possible gold medals. And until 1968, the Olympic hockey tournament was also counted as the Ice Hockey World Championship in each Olympic year, giving the tournament even higher stakes. It wasn't until the 1956 Winter Games that the Soviet Union really took over as the dominant team. The United States captured the gold once in 1960 and again in the "Miracle" 1980 Games, but the Soviet Union was considered the team to beat.

When I played in 1968, the Soviets were formidable. They had handily won all seven of their games in the 1964 Games, easily capturing the gold medal. The team was led by some incredible players—especially Anatoly Firsov, who I believe was in the top five players in the world when we faced him. Goalie Vladislav Tretiak and forwards Valeri Kharlamov, Alexander Yakushev, Vladimir Petrov, and Boris Mikhailov

My fifth birthday picture, taken at Biagini's Studio.

A few of my relatives in front of our house on Allen Street in the Soo.

My first year with the Algoma Contractors juvenile hockey team.

Our northern Ontario championship picture in 1958.

My junior year with the Gophers.

The Minnesota Gophers hockey team, 1962-63.

The St. Paul Pioneer Press *shot this picture of Francine tending to me after I fractured my cheekbone in 1963.*

Our wedding day, posing with my mom and dad, Evelyn and Mike.

I graduated in June 1963 from the University of Minnesota Business School.

Broadcasting my first Minnesota State High School Hockey Tournament in 1964.

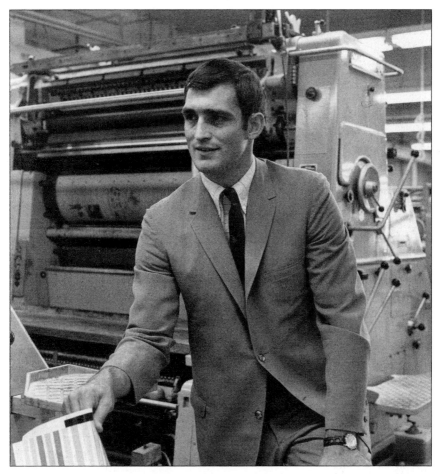

I joined the Mackay Envelope Company in 1964.

The team picture for our USHL Rochester Mustangs in 1965.

Coaching the University of Minnesota Freshmen in 1966.

were instrumental in leading the Soviet team to their heights over the next decade.

We had a good team in 1968, and it also happened to be a bunch of good guys. Our 1968 United States Olympic Team roster was:

Goaltenders: Pat Rupp and James Logue

Defensemen: Bob Paradise, Paul Hurley, Donald Ross, Bruce Riutta, Robert Gaudreau, and Lou Nanne

Forwards: Herb Brooks, Larry Pleau, John Cunniff, Doug Volmar, Leonard Lilyholm, Craig Falkman, Jack Morrison, Tom Hurley, Larry Stordahl, and Jack Dale

Coach: Murray Williamson

Eight of our players went on to play in the NHL or the WHA (World Hockey Association).

Murray Williamson was one of the most influential figures in Minnesota hockey history. He played for the Minnesota Gophers from 1957 to 1959 and was the team's MVP and an All-American in 1959. He first began coaching with the South St. Paul Steers of the USHL from 1963 to 1967, then in international competition with the U.S. National and Olympic teams in 1967, 1968, and then later from 1970 to 1972. Much later, in 2001, Murray was named one of the 50 most significant players and coaches in Minnesota Hockey history. I think we knew it even then.

Even though we played hard in the Games, we did not play as well as we could have. But it was a great time and I had the opportunity to play hockey with some great players and wonderful individuals. As the years pass, the memories of being a part of the team reaffirm that the experience was one of the major highlights of my hockey career.

I still remember Ken Broderick, the goalie for Canada, robbing me with 15 seconds to go. Canada had scored two power-play goals to take a 3–2 lead. We pulled our goalie in the last minute and

Murray put me at center. I got free in front of the net, shot for the corner, and it looked like it was going in. Then Kenny gloved it. We became teammates the next year—and he never let me forget about that play.

Herb Brooks and I were co-captains on the team and roommates. He will forever go down in hockey history as the catalyst to the great Olympic victory in 1980, but Herbie was much more than just a great hockey coach. First, he was an outstanding hockey player in his own right. He would not have been a member of the 1964 and 1968 Olympic teams otherwise! He was also an amazing person. We went through a lot together and our lifelong friendship has always meant a great deal to me. Herbie was a special person and we had some incredible times together. I miss him dearly.

Some of my memories about that Olympic year occurred *between* the hockey games that we played. In 1967 we were playing on a pre-Olympic tour of Europe. We had been playing in Switzerland and arrived in Geneva at supper time. We had played in another part of Switzerland the night before and we arrived late, so we hadn't had an opportunity to see Geneva. It was a fabulous part of the country and none of us had ever been there before. We were all excited.

Coach Williamson put a damper on things, telling us we had a 10:30 PM curfew. He was upset at our play the night before and wanted to send a strong message: we had better improve if we wanted to enjoy these fabulous parts of Europe. We were upset—especially being in a beautiful city like Geneva that none of us had seen before. Herb, trainer Doc Rose, and I went out to dinner together and discussed the curfew in some unsettling terms.

I recall Herbie saying, "Look, this is crazy. I want to go out and see this town." Doc said, "I will tell you this much, I am the trainer and I sure as hell am not going to stay in. I'm going out! I didn't play in that game and I am not going to follow that curfew!"

I wasn't convinced. I told them, "No, no, I'm not coming with you guys. Murray will check tonight and he said if anyone breaks curfew they will be sent home. I'm not going because I know he means it." And I wasn't finished either. I turned to Herbie, "We can't go! He is going to check us tonight and he will send us home." Herbie looked at me and said, "I don't care. I'm going." And Doc chimed in, "Good, because I'm going too."

The two of them went downtown after dinner. Fortunately, I had learned from the movies how to make it seem like a person was in bed sleeping. I actually became quite good at it after a few tries. I just got a pillow and some blankets and put it all together under the covers. At first glance, it looked like Herbie was in bed asleep.

And sure enough, at 10:35 PM there was a knock on the door. It was Murray Williamson doing a curfew bed-check just as I suspected he would. I had the lights out and yelled out, "What!" when I heard the knock. Murray told me to open the door, which I did partially. I told him in an angry tone, "Look, it's bad enough that you kept us in tonight but now you come around and bug us too, and won't even let us sleep. Herb is already asleep." He looked over and saw the bed with the dummy in it and said, "Okay, fine, go to sleep."

Herb and Doc came back in about 1:00 AM. I guess they had a good time. He and Doc were out enjoying the beautiful city of Geneva while I was fabricating a dummy in his bed and hiding out in the dark of our room, waiting for bed-check. Luckily, Coach Williamson must not have checked on Doc because he didn't get in trouble either.

There was another time that Herbie wanted to go again, and I agreed to go with him. We were staying at the Olympic Village in Grenoble. We had played on Sunday night and were off until Tuesday. But Coach Williamson told us that we were not allowed to leave the village.

We had nothing to do on Monday night. We had a practice on Monday afternoon and were back at the village by 6:30 in the evening, with nothing at all to do. This was too much for Herbie. He came to me and said, "Come on, we're going out. Let's go into town and have supper."

"How are we going to get out without being noticed?" I asked.

"It won't be a problem. I already found a way to get out. There is this fence in the back. We can go over it and no one will see us." That was good enough for me.

It had been raining outside and everything was wet. There were puddles everywhere and moving around was treacherous in some places. When we got to the back fence, it was pitch black outside. I went over the fence first and landed with a splat. When Herb asked me how it was, I told him it was fine. He jumped over the fence, landed in all the muck, and started screaming at me, "You ——! Why didn't you tell me to watch the mud?" Of course I wasn't going to tell him after what had just happened to me—especially after this whole disaster was his idea.

So we got our bearings, gathered ourselves together, and went into town and had dinner. We found this little Italian restaurant with two other people in there. It was Peggy Fleming, the fabulous Olympic figure skater, and her mother. I'm sure they wondered why we looked the way we did; it was nice of them not to ask. We ate and made it back to the village without any trouble, but it was quite the evening.

Actually, Herb and I had another encounter with Fleming earlier that year. It was in 1967 and we were playing our pre-Olympic schedule. We were in Colorado Springs, Colorado. Our last game was against Italy's Olympic Team and we had beaten them badly. It was New Year's Eve and Herbie, Craig Falkman, and I had decided to take our wives out to dinner. We were the only ones who had brought our spouses along to the tournament.

Herbie asked me where we should go. I told him we were going to the Penrose Room at the Broadmoor Hotel.

"I'm not going there. I can't afford that. No way!" he protested.

I told him, "Herbie, it's not a problem. Trust me, I have it all taken care of. We are guests of Thayer Tutt. He owns the Broadmoor and is the president of USA Hockey. It is all arranged."

I told Herbie that Thayer Tutt was the key person responsible for bringing the first men's NCAA Hockey Championships to the Broadmoor World Arena in Colorado Springs, Colorado. From 1966 to 1969 he was the president of the International Ice Hockey Federation and we were going to be his special guests.

So the six of us go to the Broadmoor and have a wonderful dinner. When the check came, I took it and wrote on the check, "Courtesy of Thayer Tutt, International Hockey," and added a nice tip to the dinner bill.

Herbie looks over at me and says, "Louie, wasn't that nice of him to do that for us. When did you talk to him?" I told Herb, "I never talked to him, but if you think I am missing work and paying to play on this Olympic team, you are crazy. At least we are getting a nice meal out of this whole thing, and if Thayer asks, tell him to talk to me."

We never heard a thing about it. Herbie was right. It was nice of Mr. Tutt—even if he didn't realize he was doing all this for us on New Year's Eve. Even though I expected Coach Williamson to ask who did it, we never heard a word.

We were in the lobby after dinner when the goaltender from the Italian team came over and invited us to their New Year's Eve party. He said to me, "Luigi, even though you scored on me today, I want to party with you tonight." I said okay, but told him that we had a fourth couple as well. He told us to go ahead and invite them. That fourth couple was Peggy Fleming and her boyfriend, who we were just talking to in the lobby. I had met her through her coach, Carlo Fassi, who was trying to convince me to go and play for Milan once the Olympics were over. The eight of us attended the party and had an unbelievable time. Those Italians couldn't play hockey, but were number one in entertainment in my book.

The feeling of standing on the ice with the U.S. Olympic Team is hard to translate into words. The emotion and pride of being a representative of your country is very special, and something that has meant a great deal to me. As the years go by, that feeling has only intensified. Few people ever have the opportunity to represent their country in sports, and it is truly an incredible honor. And I appreciated every minute of it.

The Olympics have been a big part of my life. When I played it meant so much to me and I know it does to every player that ever put on an Olympic uniform. Skating and playing for your country is a once in a lifetime opportunity. I only wish that everyone could experience that feeling, that internal elation, and the pride within you. Olympic participation cannot be beat. It is a dream I never dreamed but an experience I can never top.

Herb Brooks and the "Miracle" Olympics

The whole selection process for the 1980 coach and team was very special. I believe it was all meant to be. Walter Bush and I were both directly involved on the selection committee to find the coach. We pushed hard for Herb Brooks. I had just recently been named the general manager of the Minnesota North Stars and Walter had made a significant mark in hockey around the country and locally as an outstanding administrator.

I knew what he brought to the table. He was a tremendous motivator and had been a very successful coach at the college level. I wanted him to be the head coach for the North Stars. We negotiated the terms of the job for a couple of weeks before he said, "Lou, I really want to coach the Olympics. Will you help me?"

Herbie was also an exceptional judge of talent. He played an American brand of hockey that mixed a European type play of puck possession with the North American physical style and it created an exciting, fast-paced action that became the trademark of the 1980 team.

He did a fantastic job in every respect. And when the biggest game of all was over and the U.S. team had defeated the Soviets, I remember going to the locker room and finding Herbie sitting on the floor outside the door all alone. I recall the moment like it was this morning, Herbie looking up at me and saying, "Can you —— believe what just happened?"

I told him, "No, I can't believe it. It is mindboggling!"

People came from everywhere to get a look at the team. It seemed like everyone wanted to get into the locker room. I recall a guy trying to get into the locker room who waited a long time before he was eventually let in. It was Jamie Farr, the "Klinger" character from *M*A*S*H,* who just wanted to celebrate.

Upsetting the Soviets and winning the gold medal was no freak accident. It happened by design. It took a tremendous amount of hard work, and Herbie really drove the team. He knew that in order to win at the Games, he would have to develop a very different mentality. The team would have to play much tougher competition leading up to the Games. He came to me and asked to help him get a tougher pre-Olympic schedule.

He said he needed a tougher schedule than college games, and I told him we could only get him exhibition games in the NHL. Since I was chairman of the Central Pro League, I suggested we go to meet the president, Bud Poile, to see if he would fit them in our minor-league schedule. Bud was fantastic. He put them into the regular-season schedule and the games counted in the standings. This gave the Olympic Team some strong competition, since the league was composed of the top minor league teams for the National Hockey League.

I honestly never thought the U.S. team had a chance to beat the Soviet Union. I was once asked, at what point in the game did I think there was a chance to win? My response was, "When there was one second left in the game!" I never thought there was a chance to win until I saw the clock run down at the end.

The Soviets were such a great team. For the players, it was their life, their livelihood. They had tremendous passion for the game and for winning. Every player was gifted. They were unbelievable in every aspect of their game. They had outstanding goaltending and great skaters and playmakers. It was not just a hockey team. They had Vladislav Tretiak in the nets, considered by most hockey experts to be one of the greatest goalies of all time. And they had Viktor Tikhonov as their coach, no less than the builder and creator of one of the greatest dynasties in hockey history.

Tikhonov's teams practiced 10 to 11 months a year and spent most of their lives confined to barracks-type living. Their goal was to win and they almost always did. They didn't feel anyone could beat them. They were a winning machine.

There is no available comparison to the upset. But the United States team was not just a bunch of young players who were thrown together. They were a very good hockey team that Herb had hand-picked, and he had them incredibly conditioned. He made a point of being absolutely sure that his hockey team was not going to lose because they were out-conditioned. It was an excellent group of players who were trained to play well together, and on top of it all, tremendously conditioned. No one was going to outwork them and no one was going to put forth more effort—Herbie made absolutely sure of that.

If there was any question about the quality of the players' skills, all you have to do is look at what they went on to do. Many had very successful careers in the National Hockey League following the Olympic Games in 1980. Of course, nobody knew that at the time. Though Herbie did know that his group was prepared to play and they were in top physical condition.

Herb coached them to limit their mistakes. He was blessed with Jim Craig in the net. Craig was fabulous, especially in the game against the Soviets. If he hadn't been, the score would have been very different.

It had to have been disheartening for the Soviets, making one assault on the net after another, only to be turned away by Craig each time. Craig's play, along with the rest of the team's performances, just all came together. The heavens aligned for something special to happen and, well, it happened! I think that if that team had gone out and played the Soviet Union 99 more times, they might have lost them all. The Soviets were just that good of a team. But on that day, in that game, it was the U.S. who prevailed.

The Soviet team played a terrific hockey game, actually better than the U.S. But I think they made a tactical error when they replaced the great Tretiak in the goal. On top of that, I think the Soviets expected the U.S. team to quit. They didn't realize the mind-set of those kids and how mentally tough they had become.

They played as good a hockey game as they could have, and the difference in the game was Jim Craig in the nets. He just stopped everything they threw at him.

It was a terrific hockey game from beginning to end, every moment of it unforgettable. Craig undoubtedly faced more pressure in the game and perhaps later on in his professional career than most players, and I have often thought about that. How do you ever top that?

Sitting at the game, as it was drawing to a close, I remember that I could barely watch. In fact, I actually closed my eyes. I had played against many of the Soviets in the past and every time they got control of the puck I expected them to score. It was nerve-wracking. They were always able to do almost anything they wanted on the ice. But Jim Craig hung tough and his teammates were playing with a passion that was incomparable.

I was sitting right on the blue line across from the benches and the atmosphere in the arena was incredible. When the game ended, the puck was right in front of me on the ice. It was unbelievable! I kept thinking, *Did this really happen? Did we just beat the Soviet Union?* There was absolute bedlam in the building, in the streets, throughout the village—and it lasted all night long. People were just ecstatic.

It was a credit to Herb Brooks. Without him, the United States team could not have played harder or worked harder. The players had resented him back then because he had driven them so hard. He was tremendously demanding as a coach and he never let up on them. He got them ready for the Olympic Games, not just to play the Soviet team, but to beat them.

There was never a moment when Herbie didn't know what he wanted out of this team. He knew what he wanted, knew what he needed from the players and he was going to get it or kill them all in the process. He was dedicated and committed to this and was not going to back off. It was the catalyst for winning and it worked to perfection even though it was unpopular along the way.

I still keep in contact with many of the players on that dramatic team of 1980. And they all came to know and love Herbie later on. A few of them later played for me with the North Stars. They are all special and I have great admiration for them and for what they accomplished. They are a part of one of the greatest feats in American sports history.

4

The Minnesota
North Stars

L ooking back, it is impossible to fathom how my career progressed. I never did play for the Greyhounds senior team, my
onetime dream. Instead, I became a college All-American at the
University of Minnesota, played in Rochester, joined the U.S.
Olympic Team, and then went on to play for the Minnesota North
Stars in 635 National Hockey League games over a 10-year span.
Also, during my tenure with the North Stars, I was able to play for
the U.S. National Team, participating in the World Championship
tournaments in 1976 and 1977, and in the inaugural Canada Cup
in 1976.

It took some doing to get me under contract with the North
Stars. It was the urging of John Mariucci, Walter Bush, and Angelo
Bumbacco that finally got me into uniform. Finally, about a month
after the Olympics, I signed a contract to play with the North Stars.

For a quarter of a century the NHL had been a six-team league,
with franchises in Montreal, Toronto, Chicago, Detroit, Boston,
and New York. As the expansion of the league materialized, it was

quickly determined that there may not be a better place to play NHL hockey than in Minnesota, which has long been known as a true hotbed for hockey.

Walter Bush was one of the key individuals behind the effort to bring an NHL franchise to the Twin Cities. He had been known through the years for being an integral influence in the growth and development of amateur hockey in the United States. His efforts toward the success of the sport had also been significant in Minnesota, though his reputation as a major contributor toward the advancement of hockey was well known throughout the country and the world.

Walter teamed up with Bob McNulty, who had made his success in the construction business, and Gordon Ritz, a broadcasting personality, to form the primary leadership to obtain the franchise in Minnesota. Eventually there were several primary investors in the effort, John Driscoll among them.

In all, there were 14 other cities bidding for an NHL franchise— the league was creating six of them. Executives concluded that it would be a mistake to exclude a hockey-rich state like Minnesota. So, in 1967, NHL hockey finally came to the Twin Cities.

Additionally, the National Hockey League made the decision to create franchises in St. Louis, Los Angeles, Philadelphia, Pittsburgh, and Oakland.

Initially, there was no appropriate place for the new Minnesota team to take up residence. The largest local arena, the St. Paul Auditorium, housed only 8,500 spectators. Due to the success that the Minnesota Vikings and the Minnesota Twins found in Bloomington, Minnesota, it was decided that a new hockey arena would be constructed to house the hockey team next to Metropolitan Stadium. Thus the building of the Metropolitan Sports Center became a reality. It remained the home of the Minnesota North Stars for 26 years.

It didn't take long after the NHL made the decision to expand to Minnesota that a season ticket drive began, as well as a contest to find the team's new name. There were many interesting candidates considered, but the winner was the North Stars, representing the Minnesota's state nickname, the North Star State.

Yet one of the most significant decisions in franchise history was happening behind the scenes. Executives of the team named its first general manager and head coach: Wren Blair. Blair had come from the Boston Bruins organization. Wren had some local ties, as he once served as the coach and general manager of the Minneapolis Bruins, who played then in the Central Professional Hockey League as an affiliate of the Boston franchise.

Wren Blair, who was known as "Bird," always seemed to have a smile on his face. He was the classic showman, perhaps one of the best ever. He was the perfect fit. Flamboyant, demonstrative, and extremely outspoken, he brought considerable attention to the team from the media and the general public.

Wren and I coexisted. I have no doubt in my mind that he did not like the fact that I was popular here in the Twin Cities. I had enjoyed three very successful years playing hockey for the Minnesota Gophers and then became a member of the U.S. Olympic Team, serving as the captain of both teams. In addition, I had several successful seasons playing for Rochester

"Wren Blair was upset because of all the local publicity Louie received. As a part of his personal services contract with the North Stars, Louie was working for me selling advertising for the game programs. The advertisers, in turn, wanted Louie in their promotion ads. So the first program we put out had Louie's picture in the program in eight places. Blair put a stop to that real quick!"

—Tom Colwell, former boss and longtime friend

(Minnesota) in the United States Hockey League. In joining the North Stars, I really solidified my connection to Minnesota hockey and its die-hard hockey community. I know that struck a negative chord with Blair because I also got a lot of attention from fans and the media.

As a coach, I liked Wren for the most part. We got along the majority of the time, but that issue was always there right under the surface. He liked to control his players and I think he didn't have the kind of control over me he would have liked. After all, I already knew the principal investors in the team!

We also had some friction when it came to my actions on the ice. He would try to motivate me or irritate me—sometimes I wasn't sure which—by telling me that someone was going to take my job. I recall him once saying to me, "Nanne, we have drafted a kid out of western Canada who is going to take your job from you." As one might imagine, it didn't sit well with me when he did that. As far as I was concerned, no one was going to take my job. So when Wren used that kind of tactic with me, I had a few things to say to him. I knew that the one thing completely under my own control was the effort that I put forth. I had always known that there might be better players with more skills and ability than I had, but there would never be a player who would ever outwork me.

So when Wren threatened my job, I came back to him with, "Wren, I will tell you this. You are in total control and I can't do anything about your decision, but I ask you to just do one thing."

He looked at me and said, "What would that be?"

I told him, "Let the competition on the ice determine who is going to play and who isn't going to play. Don't make a decision about who is going to play just because you picked some player in the draft or traded for someone, because I will outwork him! Let the competition on the ice determine who is going to play."

I appreciate the fact that Wren listened to what I had to say, because that is exactly what happened. I outworked the kid from western Canada, and my job remained mine. Occasionally, Coach would come to me and tell me he was going to trade me. I would say, "Go right ahead. Why don't you send me to Detroit?" He said, "You'd like that, wouldn't you?" I said, "Yes I would." He said, "I'm not trading you, you'll probably play 10 years in this league." There's one thing Wren was right about.

> *"Louie was the type of player that made himself a good hockey player. He never took a night off. He was there to play every game."*
>
> —J.P. Parise, former teammate, Minnesota North Stars

The amount of effort put forth is the one thing that every player has the ability to control in hockey. As a player, you will not be able to control the skills and abilities of another player, but you do have the ability to give your full effort, every time. No one can ever take that away from you.

Wren Blair had never played the game but he did have a very good eye for talent. He had been a scout, and although he may not have been the very first person to marvel at the ability of Bobby Orr, he can take full credit for signing Orr to a Boston contract when the player was only 14 years old. They would sign youngsters to a "C" form in those days, and the NHL club that owned the Junior team would own a player's rights.

Blair was also very good at getting space in the newspaper and was outstanding at promoting the newly formed Minnesota North Stars franchise. He was very good for the franchise and did a good job overall, mostly because he was such a terrific promoter. He would make outrageous statements, and he never hesitated to bait sportswriters with his commentary.

He didn't feel that the Minnesota public was very educated about hockey; he was convinced they weren't sure when to clap or boo during a game. He felt he had to educate them and worked hard at getting Minnesota fans interested in the game.

Blair had a tremendous desire and ambition to be successful and he went to great lengths to get there. But we players did not like him and at times banded together against him. As I look back on those days, Wren probably planned it that way in order to bring the team together. He was a master at that type of motivation.

Because he was both coach and general manager, he had a great measure of control over the team. He was tough with contract negotiations and regularly sent players up and down from the North Stars to the minor leagues. There was no doubt it was an interesting and exciting time for the new franchise, yet it was often unsettling for the players, uncertain of what was in store for us.

When the new teams came in to the National Hockey League an expansion draft was conducted. The Original Six teams were able to protect 11 skaters and one goalie. Blair exercised his drafting option by taking my friend, Cesare Maniago, as our goalie.

Cesare was familiar to the fans in the Twin Cities because he had played for the Minneapolis Bruins in the Central Hockey league. Overall, Wren set the tone for the organization by building a strong offensive team, including players such as Wayne Connelly, Dave Balon, and Bill Goldsworthy. It was an exciting time for hockey in the state of Minnesota. The fans came out in support of the team—and Wren was enjoying every minute of it.

With the expansion teams now in competition with the established teams, the league set up two divisions; the East Division housed the original teams and the West Division composed of the new franchises. Playoffs were set within each division, and the two division winners met to compete for the Stanley Cup. It was a great time for professional hockey, even though the new franchises had a tough time beating the established teams when they met in the Stanley Cup Finals.

It is hard to imagine, looking at the 30 teams playing in the NHL today, that at one time, for a player to fulfill a dream of playing in the NHL, he had to be skilled enough to make the roster of one of only six teams.

During my years playing with the North Stars, I was primarily used as a defenseman, although I did play some as a forward. My best season was 1971–72, when I scored 21 goals and had 28 assists for 49 points at right wing.

The first game I ever played for the North Stars was against St. Louis. It had been a little over a month since the Olympics had ended. In that first NHL game, I played five positions on the ice; I felt as if my body might never recover.

During my career, I became the only player to play in each of the North Stars' first 11 seasons. By 1978, I knew my playing career was coming to an end. Happily, I was very fortunate to be named coach and general manager of the North Stars.

It was never my desire to coach the team. Initially, I went after Herb Brooks for the job. Herbie refused, and I was still looking when North Stars and the Cleveland Barons merged at draft time in the spring. I ended up as coach on February 10, 1978, and coached until the end of the season.

I hired Harry Howell to coach in the following season, but after just one month, he developed a heart condition. So he instead took over as our director of player personnel and I put Glen Sonmor in as our head coach.

My stint as the general manager of the North Stars was exciting and invigorating for me. I was determined to make the North Stars a winning team, and I gave every ounce of my energy, my heart, and my soul to that job for the next 10 years. I had loved every minute of the game as a player—now I had the opportunity to make decisions about every aspect of the team's operations.

It was a difficult job from the first day that I took it on. What I didn't know at the time was how the job would affect me. I had always had some obsessive-compulsive behavior in my life, and I demonstrated it often as a player. Putting on my skates a certain way, my elbow pads a certain way, always following Bill Goldsworthy out of the locker room—those kinds of things. Superstitions, as we called them. But as it turned out, it was much more than that for me. I know I inherited some of the traits from my dad.

From as far back as I can remember, I would always do things to the extremes. Even as a youngster I was very set in my ways—especially before a game. I would have to eat the same food at the same time at the same place. As I got older, my obsessions got worse as the intensity in my life increased. By the time I was general manager of the North Stars, my obsessive-compulsive disorder was out of control.

As a player with the North Stars, I had plenty of obsessions, but becoming general manager and taking on so many more responsibilities led to a significant change in my life. My desire to win was overwhelming.

When I started in my new role as the general manager of the Minnesota North Stars, we were in dead last. I wanted to do something about that, and began my efforts to build a Stanley Cup championship team. There was never one single minute or second when I forgot that ultimate goal.

The best part the job was building what would become tremendous friendships with the general managers of other NHL franchises. There was a special camaraderie that we developed, and it will stay with me for the rest of my life. Today, it's the only part of the job that I miss. The bond that many of us had was similar to a brotherhood. As much as we wanted to defeat each other's teams on the ice—and we would have gone to any lengths to do so—our kinship was still something special that we shared.

I think a lot of it had to do with the understanding of what the others had to go through in order to be successful. It was tough work, and there was tremendous pressure on each of us to win. Winning was what it was all about and accomplishing that was no easy task.

I spent a great deal of time with Cliff Fletcher, Bill Torrey, Glen Sather, Pat Quinn, Bob Pulford, and Harry Sinden, as well as the Esposito brothers, Phil and Tony, who I have known my entire life. These were general managers that I spent most of my time with at meetings and always found

> *"Louie enjoys life and hockey more than anyone I know."*
>
> —CLIFF FLETCHER, TORONTO MAPLE LEAFS SENIOR ADVISER AND FORMER NHL GENERAL MANAGER

opportunities to be with them when I got the chance to do so. It was wonderful, and we are all good friends. But make no mistake about it—I wanted to beat them every chance I got.

When I first started in the role as a general manager, I can honestly say that I was not very well prepared to do the job. I had been a player and this was very different for me. One day I was a player just like everyone else on the team, and the next day I was the boss.

Shortly after I became GM, I met with the team and told them, "I really enjoyed playing with all of you and I consider you all my friends. And I hope we can continue to be friends. But my friendship with you will not stop me from doing what I think needs to be done to improve this hockey team. I may feel the need to make decisions that may be hurtful and I'm sorry for that. I know that I am going to have to do some things that some of you will not like, but through it all I hope we can still be friends."

It was a tough thing to do. One of my first actions as GM was to trade Doug Hicks. Doug and I used to ride together. We were close. The decision was difficult but it had to be done. I had resolved never to be afraid or hesitant to make the moves that I felt were right for the team. And unfortunately, Doug made a great deal of money and our budget was very tight.

My philosophy was, if someone did not want to play for the North Stars, we had to find a way to move him. I only wanted players that wanted to be in Minnesota and be a part of our team. The hardest trade I ever had to make was Bobby Smith. In his case, I waited longer after he asked to be traded than I would have normally because I hoped that he would change his mind and continue his career with the North Stars. He never did, and I eventually traded him.

When I was a player, I never wanted to be traded. I thought everyone should feel the same way. Unfortunately, there were plenty of guys who did not. And if someone came into my office and asked to leave, I traded them.

I recall a player once coming into my office saying, "Either coach Glen Sonmor goes or I go!" I looked up at him and said, "Where do you want to go? I'll try to accommodate you."

When I made a trade, it was always my practice to call the player into my office and tell him personally. My first trade, with Doug Hicks, was tough. I told him, "Doug, I have an opportunity to get a forward here who is a good potential scorer. Our budget is way out of whack and you make a lot of money. I have to trade you. It is not something I want to do but I have to do it." He was certainly surprised, but he handled it very well, like a real professional.

My first few years as general manager were quite successful. We had been in last place and soon made it in the playoffs. It helped us somewhat when we merged with the Cleveland team that had folded but less so than some people thought.

I remember Sam Pollock, the Montreal Canadiens general manager, saying, "Don't worry about those North Stars merging with Cleveland. When you take one bag of —— and merge it with another bag of ——, all you get is one bigger bag of ——."

We also had some successful drafts my first few years. Our biggest early acquisitions included Bobby Smith as our first pick and then later on, Steve Payne. Both turned out to be tremendous players for the North Stars. We also had two excellent players in the same draft in Curt Giles and Steve Christoff.

Others joined us later, including Neal Broten, Brian Bellows, Dino Ciccarelli, and Mike Modano—all outstanding players who really contributed through the years to make the franchise exciting. Of course, there were many others that made the North Stars an entertaining hockey team.

We drafted good players to go with what we had and were always on the move to improve the team in any way possible. Before long, we not only made the playoffs but got to the Stanley Cup finals in 1981, before losing in five games to a great New York Islanders team.

We had some very good seasons and got very close, but we never were able to make it to the top of the mountain and capture that ultimate dream of winning the Stanley Cup. That goal will forever elude me. It has always bothered me that we never got there.

As the general manager, you make good trades and you make bad trades; you have good player drafts and you have bad player drafts. It is all a part of the constant effort to make your team better. One of the things at which I worked very hard at drafting player contracts. I was the only general manager at the time to have signed only one player to a one-way contract during my whole 10-year career. The rest of my contracts were two-way. Under a two-way contract, if a player stayed in the NHL, they were paid a set amount, but if they were sent down to the minor leagues, their salary was reduced accordingly. Most teams signed many players to a contract that called for the same salary whether they were playing in the NHL or the minors. The only player I ever signed to a one-way contract was Bobby Smith, and he never disappointed me. At the time we signed him, we were battling the WHA for his rights. We had no alternative but to give him a one-way deal.

All contracts in the National Hockey League are guaranteed. When a player is signed, they are paid for the life of the contract— even if they are released or injured. I was never concerned about what I paid someone on the upside of a contact. If someone played in the NHL and collected their salary for doing their job, that was fine with me. But I didn't want to pay someone that same amount and have them playing in the minor leagues.

It was very important to me to make budget, and I didn't intend to spend a lot of money on someone who wasn't even on the North Stars roster. It just made good common sense. In all my years as general manager, I never had a year over budget.

Once I was traveling with the president of the Quebec Nordiques, Marcel Aubut. We were discussing player contracts and I told him that he was paying his players too much money. He said he was sure that we were all paying essentially the same money. I had my contract book with me and pulled it out and showed him what we were doing with the North Stars. He couldn't believe it. He asked me how much money I was making as the general manager of the North Stars. I told him $85,000 per year. Right there on the spot, he told me, "I will pay you $85,000 per year to just do the contracts for Quebec." I laughed, but it further convinced me that I was doing things correctly.

When we drafted Brian Bellows in the first round, he signed a two-way contract. Later, when negotiating the contract for first-round pick Brian Lawton, his agent wanted a one-way contract. The agent said he had heard Bellows had one in the year he was drafted. I told him he was wrong, and we actually made a bet about it. Because the contracts were private, I got permission from the league for him to look at Bellows' contract. I won the bet and he bought me dinner at Bigliardi's in Toronto. In today's era, the majority of the players have one-way contracts, although the two-way contract still exists for some of the younger and first-year players. I'm convinced it was that system that allowed our team to stay within budget so consistently.

My budgetary goals were very important to me. First of all, I worked for two great owners in George and Gordon Gund, both brilliant businessmen. Working for them was the equivalent to getting a Harvard education. They really developed my business acumen. Plus, I had my own educational background of University of Minnesota business school to draw on, as well as my earlier training with Harvey Mackay and Tom Colwell. And before all that, I had what I learned from my parents. After all, my mother ran a clothing store and my dad ran a grocery store, so I learned a great deal about management, expenses, and the bottom line from my own family.

I learned to always pay special attention to the downside of a deal, believing that the upside would take care of itself. And for the most part, it did. I knew where every penny went. My commitment to accuracy and consistency and my winning philosophy is just a part of who I am. Now you take that pressure inherent in the job and then combine that with feelings present in me, you can only imagine how I felt when we won—and how I felt when we lost.

I always had great admiration for those in the general manager ranks who could keep things balanced, no matter the outcome of the games. Glen Sather was one who kept things in perspective. Doug Risebrough, former general manager of the Wild, is another. Many others were able to stay on somewhat of an even keel through the good times and the bad times; I simply could not do that. I marveled at Bill Torrey's composure, the calmness of Cliff Fletcher and Glen Sather, the consistency of Harry Sinden's teams, the firmness of Bob Pulford, and the competitiveness of Emile Francis.

When we won, I would be completely exhilarated. When we lost I would be really down. Even if the game we had played had

"Even though we have been rivals for many years, we have always had a great relationship. He has been an excellent hockey man. He has done a great deal for USA Hockey, the University of Minnesota, the Olympic Team, and the National Hockey League. He has been on countless committees to improve the game."

—HARRY SINDEN, FORMER GENERAL MANAGER, BOSTON BRUINS

little consequence in the standings, it didn't matter. I suffered greatly with the losses. It was overwhelming, pure devastation—and I did everything I could to prevent them from happening.

Sometimes after a loss I would sit in my office until 4:00 in the morning trying to figure out what went wrong. It just ate me up inside and out. I would sit there and do nothing. I could not move forward. I could not come to grips with it. I was paralyzed.

I recall my brother and sister visiting us from Canada for a game we played against Detroit. We had been ahead 3–0 in the third period. Detroit then went on to score three times so the game ended in a tie. I was devastated.

They sat with me in my office until 1:00 in the morning and I never said one thing to them, not one word. I just sat there. They had some conversation with my wife but not a solitary word from me. It was awful the way I behaved, but the tie score just killed me after we had that big lead late in the game.

Finally we went home and they sat around visiting for a little while, and I went to bed. I could not have been ruder to them, but I couldn't help myself. The next day my brother told me, "Louie, we should have just stayed in Sault Ste. Marie, as much as we talked to you!" I told him, "I can't help it. I wish I could have, but I'm really upset over what happened last night." That's what would happen to me after a loss; it was something I simply could not control.

As time went on, it worsened. In fact, at one point it got so bad that I ended up on *The Oprah Winfrey Show* to talk about my compulsive behavior.

On the nights when we won, I relished in the triumph. I enjoyed every minute of it. It was fantastic in every respect. I can still remember sitting on a bus with the North Stars after a big win in St. Louis in my rookie year as a player. We were off to a good start that year and had won four or five games in a row. I was on a real high. I can remember thinking, *Wow, this is really something! Nothing could ever be better than this!* I recall thinking how much fun I was having playing on a good team, being on a winning streak, having just won another game.

That feeling I had then seems so vivid, even now. There wasn't any better feeling in the world. A win would do that for me. It was at the core of my very being.

Those tremendous highs got bigger once I stepped into the general manager's role. I would become incredibly overjoyed with a victory. That it in itself was a contributing factor to the despair that I felt with a loss. I could never understand how some of my fellow GMs took losing in stride. There was so much joy in success and so much desolation in failure. Being able to handle things on an even keel was something I never could do. I envied those who could.

I tried very hard to keep my work separate from my home life. It didn't always work—including the day when my brother and sister had come in for the game—but for the most part I was successful. I wouldn't allow my kids to talk about the game or the team. I told them, "We don't talk hockey at home. Enjoy the game, have a good time, but I don't want to come home and then start talking about the game again."

Home had to be my safe haven. And if we weren't going to talk about the losses, we wouldn't talk about the wins, either. I didn't feel like

I could handle it at work all day and then at home again at night. I was better at home keeping it that way, forgetting the pressures of my job.

My wife, Francine, and I have been together all of our lives. She understands who I am, which I have always appreciated. She has always accepted my ups and downs. She is our rock and has always kept things intact at home. Through all the peaks and valleys, she has remained steady.

I couldn't find a way to keep the losses from feeling personal. Losing bothered me so much, I couldn't help it. My mind would spin over and over—*What did we do wrong? What can we do differently? What can I do to make a difference?* It drove me crazy. I *had* to find ways to win.

Having the opportunity to work with Glen Sonmor, Murray Oliver, and J.P. Parise for so many years really ameliorated things. Glen was really good for me. He is a very upbeat and confident human being who could always find a way to settle me down.

Glen was our coach from 1979 to 1983 (and a couple other times along the way). He believed we were going to win, and he made me believe it—even during some of the roughest stretches that we went through.

Glen would always look at the positives. He, along with Murray, J.P., and John Mariucci, could also discuss things heatedly with me, and when it was over, it was over. We'd all feel good about the discussion and move on with our work; nothing ever got to the media.

I was also a firm believer in never making disparaging remarks about the players to the media. You must understand that the players on your team are your assets, so why would you want to devalue them publicly in the newspaper or other media? Also, we might trade the player someday. How could you expect to get a lot in a trade for the player if you have been ripping him in the press? It didn't make good business sense.

I always told the players, "Don't ever tell the media that you played badly. Don't ever tell them that you should have done this or you should have done that. Why confirm something for them that they may suspect? Let them figure it out. Make them do their jobs." I also told the players if they said negative things about themselves to the press, they might get fans to turn on them or start looking for them to make mistakes.

As the general manager I would talk to the team from time to time. I might have the meeting after a practice, before or after a game—whenever the timing was right and I felt I needed to say something. Usually I

"When I think of Louie, the first thing that comes to mind is someone who is honest, intelligent, and very aggressive. Of all the people that I have known in my life, I have never had more fun with anyone than I have had with Lou Nanne."

—Murray Oliver, former teammate, Minnesota North Stars

waited until my disposition reached the boiling point before I did. Oftentimes my conversations with them had to do with effort. I could not stand it if I didn't see good effort from each player all the time. I would tell them that if it didn't change, they would be sitting in some other team's locker room, because here with the North Stars, it is unacceptable. Glen would add, "You can continue to play like that, just not for the North Stars."

I have always had a complete understanding that another player might be better than you, but there is no excuse for that player to outwork you. And if that happens, there is something wrong and it needs fixing. And if we lost because we got outworked, then I had a serious problem. A team or a player may be better than you, and I accept that (though it doesn't mean I have to like it!). But I simply would not tolerate a lack of effort. I didn't accept it in myself and I was not about to accept it when it came to my team.

Having been a part of the game for most of my life, I fully understand that you can come to the rink some days and not play well. It happens to everyone. There is no way that anyone can be on top of his game all the time. But the one thing that you can give every time you play is effort.

When the New York Islanders beat us in the Stanley Cup Finals, they were better than us. They had more skilled players with more ability and it showed on the ice. As much as that series still haunts me with disappointment, I can be comfortable with it to some extent. As hard as we worked and as well as we played, it wasn't enough. We had already upset three teams and it was tough for us to do the fourth.

Whatever your job, people expect that effort from you. It applies to everything you do. In the working world, if you are paid a salary, your employer expects you to perform. And in order to perform at high levels, your best effort is the key.

Everybody has to earn their salaries. This philosophy has carried me through my business life. I tell my employees the same thing. Make sure that you earn your paycheck every day. Someone may be better than you but you can outwork them. At the end of the day, the person that works the hardest enjoys it the most and is the most successful. Because he knows that he has earned his keep.

In hockey, it is simple to determine whether a team is playing with intensity or not. You can tell easily when there is a loose puck. It's the manner in which they go after the puck or the opposing player. It can be their play around the net. But it is always quite easy to recognize.

Everyone wants players on their team that want to win and give an effort every day that they're on the ice. In addition, I always wanted to have a team skilled in the fundamentals.

I used to say to Glen Sonmor, "We have to put together a team that can play the game whichever way our opponents want us to play, so we can win at any style of the game. We need to be able to control the physical game and we need to be able to have great balance so we can always match up well with whoever we are playing. We need players who give great effort. We need toughness and we need skill." Good teams can play any game that you want—and the best teams will beat you at every one.

In some respects, as I look back on our teams, I think I may have gotten a little carried away with too many skilled players. As a result, we lacked the intensity needed at times. I recall one time, when we were going through a bad stretch, a fan called me up on the phone and said, "Mr. Nanne, I am not going to buy any more tickets because you guys are absolutely terrible!"

I said to the caller, "Do you go to movies?" He said he did. So I said to him, "Well, if you go to movies, you know that there is only one movie that will win the Oscar for the Best Picture, yet you still go to see movies, right?"

Again he said, "Yes," puzzled by my line of questioning. I said to him, "The team that wins the game must be pretty good, so keep coming to the games, and just watch the other team!"

During the 1986–87 season, I had been in the general manager's role for nine years and it was really eating at me. The day-to-day pressures of the job were closing in on me. One night, a season ticket holder, a very successful businessman and friend, Noel Rahn, approached me in the Observatory Club and said to me, "Louie, are you tired of seeing your name in the papers yet? Why don't you come out and make some real money? Come and work for me. I have just the job for you."

Noel was in finance and went on to explain his business to me. He gave me his pitch. I told him, "Noel, I appreciate your interest in me and it sounds exciting. Maybe someday I will consider it." At that particular time, I wasn't ready to make the change—but I was getting close. Still, it was nice to have his offer as an option in the back of my mind.

At the time we had that conversation, I was really suffering. I had lost weight and was not feeling well. I had taken a trip to the Mayo Clinic and had gotten a battery of tests. At the end of it all, they told me that my personality was affecting my ability to handle the stress of my job. I was told that if I continued what I was doing, I had about two years before I would start to really see some negative changes in my physical health. The upshot was basically, *change your behavior or change your job.*

I tried to be less intense. I tried to be more laid back. I tried not to get so upset over the losses and the injuries. I gave it my best shot. It didn't work. Pretty soon the stress and my personality locked horns again and I was miserable.

> *"You can always count on Lou as a friend. He will never let you down. He understands loyalty and will always be there if you need him. 'Genuine' is a great word to describe him. He is a genuine friend with a tremendous personality and great people skills."*
>
> —Noel Rahn, longtime friend

All of my superstitions and obsessions had emerged in full force. I was trying everything to win. If we won one night then I would do everything the next day that I had done before the previous game in hopes of winning again. I would take the same route to work, listen to the same radio station, drive in the same lane, eat the same meal at the same time, hold my fork a certain way, and on and on. It was endless. It was pure craziness but I had to do it. It was the only way to get my mind right.

Then one day I got a call from *The Oprah Winfrey Show*. They wanted me to come on the program and talk about superstitions. Apparently my reputation preceded me. They told me they had a clipping service and had read about my superstitions and were interested in having me discuss them. I agreed and went to Chicago for the show. I thought it might be interesting and it was—but for different reasons that I expected.

There were several people who were scheduled to appear on the show, and some of them went out on stage before me. I was waiting in the green room with a female basketball coach, and we were watching the show on the monitor. I noticed that they were not really discussing superstitions but rather obsessive-compulsive behavior. The more I listened, the more I realized that my problem was OCD. It hit me like a thunderbolt, *What I have is obsessive-compulsive disorder, not just a bunch of superstitions.*

I turned to the basketball coach and said, "That's us. That's what we have—obsessive-compulsive disorder." The coach protested, "No, I'm not like that at all." I fired back, "Yes you are and so am I! We are just like that. We must have OCD."

When I got back home, I made an appointment to see a psychiatrist and he wrote me a prescription. So I took the pills for a while and they had a relaxing effect on me. Later that week we played the Washington Capitals and I was sitting in the Observatory Club before the game. David Poile, the Capitals' very successful general manager came over to me and said, "Louie, what is going on with you? I have never seen you so relaxed before a game. What's happening?"

I reached in my pocket and pulled out the pills and told David, "These are OCD pills that I'm taking." He said to me, "Wow, give me some!" I said to him, "No, you're not getting any, go get your own! These are my new secret weapons."

So I continued on with the pills for a couple of months and things were a little better. One day I asked myself, *What am I doing? I have to take pills to do my job. This isn't right. Nothing good can come from this.* And with that, I quit taking the pills.

It wasn't very long before everything started mounting up on me again. By the time a game would come, I was suffering through all sorts of crazy behaviors. I would have to dress a certain way. I would have to hold the phone a certain way. I would walk to the press box on the same route. I would walk around a chair four times one way and then four times another way. There were so many things going on in my head that my mind was just spinning in every direction—and every bit of it was connected to winning.

It was bizarre, but I couldn't stop it. It was my way of getting my mind settled and convincing myself that we would have the best chance to win. I thought if I did things a certain way we could win. After all, it had worked before. If we lost, then I would change my behavior and try something different.

I had always behaved this way to some degree, but those tendencies progressed as the pressures of the job got greater. Even today, I still have some of it. If I happen to tap the table, then I have to tap it again with the other hand. If I tap three times with one hand, then I have to tap three times with the other hand. It's just the way I am.

I might be watching a baseball game on television and let's say a Twins batter has two strikes on him. I might switch the channel and then switch it back so he doesn't strike out. I don't have any idea if it works, in fact I truly know it has no effect on whether the batter strikes out or hits a home run. It's goofy—I know that—but I do it anyway.

When I finally did change jobs, Francine said to me, "Are you going to be the same now that you're in another job?" I said to her, "No I'm not, but I reserve the right to revert." And sometimes I still do.

Today in the financial business, I am better because I don't have to rely on it as much. I think all of this behavior likely starts with being superstitious. I know my longtime friend and hockey great Phil

Esposito has some of it. He would go nuts if he saw crossed sticks in the locker room. We all had some of these kinds of behaviors. I just got worse and it never let up as the pressures to win got greater and greater.

I understand that I cannot affect what may happen on the ice by enacting certain kinds of behaviors, but what I was doing was aligning my mind-set so that I felt we would have a better chance to win. I don't know if that makes any sense, but it is the way that I look at it. I have to have everything right in my mind to make certain the team wins. I need to get my mind comfortable with the task at hand by wearing the right clothes, driving the same way to work, eating the same way, and myriad other things.

As much as I loved the competitive aspects of being a general manager, the wins and losses were just too much. It was a difficult job and, as I mentioned, especially with the losses. I never could get away from wondering what I could do to improve the team.

One of the tactics that any general manager could use to improve his club was through trades. I earned a reputation for making a lot of them. I've already explained that I have always been willing to shed a player who didn't want to play for the North Stars. Those trades were easy. I never wanted to have a player on my team who didn't want to be there. It was the other deals that required more consideration. It was often difficult to know if I was making the right trade for the right reason.

The most difficult one I ever made, the one trade that still bothers me to this day, was Bobby Smith. Bobby was a great player, the face of our franchise, and an even better person. Bobby played for us for six years and then with the Montreal Canadiens for seven years before returning to Minnesota at the end of his career.

Bobby scored 357 career goals and recorded 679 assists for an overall total of 1,036 points in the NHL. I would have never chosen to trade Bobby, but he came to me in the winter of 1983 and asked to be traded. I was really shocked and tried to talk him out of it.

Francine and I were at the All-Star Game in New York and we were out for dinner with Gordon Gund, Harold Ballard, and their wives. I can still see exactly where we were sitting in the restaurant. Bobby and his agent, Art Kaminsky, approached our dinner table and asked to talk with me. Art told me Bobby wanted to be traded and my first reaction was, "You have got to be kidding me! It's not going to happen. Don't even think about it." I told them to enjoy themselves and I went back to the table to eat.

In October of that year Bobby came to me again with the request. "Louie, you have been putting me off for six months," he told me, "and I'm not going to take it any longer. I want the trade. You signed me to a contract for a lot of money. Your brother and my brother went to school together. They both have professional careers. If you don't trade me, I am going to retire and go back to school myself."

I tried to talk him out of it again. "Give it some time," I told him. "Let's talk again in December." Bobby said to me, "The only thing that is going to change is that I will be back here again in December wearing galoshes."

He wanted to be traded because he felt that he was not getting enough playing time. I leave that decision up to the head coach. In Bobby's mind, he was not getting enough ice time and in the coach's mind, he was. Therein lay the problem.

So I had to trade him—and it really hurt. He was the first player I ever drafted and he was a real star. Usually when you trade a player it is because you are thinking you are going to better your club; that certainly wasn't the case with Bobby. In fact, before he approached me about the trade, I had never once given a thought to trading him in all of the years he was with us. He was great for the community and great to have on the team. He was the type of player that you want with your organization forever. At the time I was trying to make the deal, I kept asking myself, *How is it possible that I can ever come out ahead on this trade? Who could I get for our team that would be better than Bobby Smith?*

In the end, it was an okay deal. Bobby made a significant impact with Montreal and we got two good players in Keith Acton and Mark Napier. We also received a second-round draft pick in the deal. Acton played especially well for us. And Bobby, well, he was just a great player and wound up winning a Stanley Cup with the Canadiens. As much as the trade bothered me, I was very happy for Bobby and the success he had in Montreal.

Trades are a very interesting part of hockey. Most general managers have their own trade philosophy, and I certainly had mine. There are some who cannot pull the trigger on a trade because they have an attitude toward the concept. *What if it doesn't work out? What if the trade is a bust? What if the player you trade becomes a superstar player for the other team?* All those questions and thoughts ruin a deal.

My philosophy is different than that. I have always felt that if you can make a trade for a player and that player performs better than the player leaving, then it has been a good trade. Once I traded a player, I didn't care how he played somewhere else (with the exception of Bobby Smith, of course!). I only cared that we improved our team by making the trade. I never felt I had the time to worry about the other player and his performance.

Some players need a change of scenery; they might go to another team and become a terrific player. I am fine with that but it scares off some general managers from making trades. I only worried about who was coming to us, not who was leaving.

I also had another philosophy about trades. I never let a coach talk to me about trading a player after the end of a game. Emotions were always too high. I would tell them, "Wait a day or so, and then if you still feel that way, we can talk about it." I never wanted a player's performance in a single game to have an effect on the coach's judgment. No good decision could come out of it.

In fact, I would sometimes call a general manager after a game when I knew their team had played badly or a certain player had not played well. I knew it might be an opportune time to make a deal with that team or for a particular player when their judgment might be somewhat clouded. It might be a good time to strike a deal when they were ripe to make an emotional mistake. These general managers of other teams were my friends, of course, but I wanted to beat them in the worst way—and believe me, they wanted the same.

I never made a trade without talking to my coaches and my scouts first. I remember receiving a call from Gump Worsley, who had been scouting up in Sherbrooke, Quebec. He said that someone had told him that the North Stars had made a certain trade and he was calling to see if it was true. I said to him, "Gump, how long have you known me? You have worked for me for nine years now. Have I ever made a trade without talking to you first?" Gump's response was "No." So I told him, "Now go and tell your so-called expert source that he is full of ——, because it didn't happen!" Gump said, "That's what I told the smartass when he talked about the trade."

It was extremely important to me to get the feedback of my coaches and scouts. Maybe one of them had something to say that I hadn't thought about in planning out the process. I would be the one making the final decision, but I trusted it would be a better decision with everyone involved. I never wanted to surprise any of my staff, plus I really relied on their experience and expertise.

Trades can happen at any time. One year, we were in training camp in Bismarck, North Dakota, playing an exhibition game. We had drafted a young kid named Ron Meighan in the first round.

Early on in camp, I just didn't like the way he was performing. Defensively, we needed a physical defenseman, and he was more of an offensive one. He was the 13th overall pick in the draft, but I knew early on that we were going to have to move him. All of the coaches and scouts were in North Dakota with me and I told them that I didn't feel this kid was going to help this year and that I was going to try to trade him. Some of my staff wanted to give him more time but I just didn't think he was going to work out so I made up my mind to move him.

Obviously, making the decision that you are going to trade someone and actually doing it are two different things. There are times, for one reason or another, when a deal does not work out to everyone's liking, and the trade is never made. Or in some cases, it takes longer to materialize than you would like.

In this case, I started thinking, *Who can I trade him to?* I knew that I wanted to get a high draft pick in return so I wanted him to go to a team that I believed would finish very low in the standings. Therefore we would get a high pick, which I would receive as a part of the deal. I started working three teams in the league where I felt fairly comfortable that they would end up with less points than us at the end of the season, and that had a good chance to actually finish quite low. Where a team finished determined its place in the draft. The higher you finished, the lower the pick you received.

I wanted to swap our pick for their pick and give them the kid in the deal. I made the trade with Pittsburgh, and Pittsburgh ended up finishing in last place. So we wound up with the first pick in the draft and took Brian Lawton. The pick we traded them was 15th in the draft, so it turned out to be a great opportunity for us.

Lawton played well but didn't work out nearly as well as it would have had we taken Pat LaFontaine or Steve Yzerman. Lawton was actually the first American-born hockey player to be taken No. 1 in the entry draft. Brian had a solid NHL career and is formerly the executive vice president and general manager of the Tampa Bay Lightning.

Anytime that I was going to trade draft picks, I would always do a thorough analysis of the teams that I might trade with to be sure they would finish lower than us. Once I made up my mind to make a deal, I never entertained any second thoughts.

Another thing you have to keep in mind in making trades is that the other general managers are smart. They didn't get into their positions by making dumb decisions. So sometimes when a deal is made, it can turn out to benefit both teams.

When we picked Brian Lawton first in the draft he had tremendous skills. We anticipated that he was going to grow considerably and we wanted a big center to help us challenge the Islanders for the Stanley Cup. They had Bryan Trottier and we wanted someone to match him in size on the ice. We felt that someday in the near future it would be Lawton. Brian's father was a big man and we thought Brian would grow to be the size of his dad, but he didn't. In fact, he is about the same size now as he was when we drafted him. He never got to the size that we expected.

The NHL entry draft was something that we prepared for all year long. We had scouts for the team scouting players all over the United States, Canada, and Europe. There is no question in my mind that the scouts are the real unsung heroes in the game. They have a very difficult job. They are on the road all the time looking at players and trying to determine if they are good enough, big enough, fast enough. They are looking for playmaking ability, skating ability, stick handling, shooting, defensive skills, physical skills, toughness, and good citizenship.

Scouts go everywhere—cold, damp, and sometimes poorly lit arenas. They drive in bad weather across lonely prairies to see a kid who sometimes doesn't even end up playing that night. It is a job I never wanted to do but it is crucial to every team. I honestly don't know how they do it. No one is more committed to the game than those individuals.

In the past, scouts never made a lot of money. They were in different cities every day of the week and at a game every night of the week. On top of the travel and games, they have a lot of work—they make notes on players, fill out reports, and talk to people about the players that are of interest. They not only gauge the player's ability but try to also determine the type of person they are.

Scouts might find a player who stands out in their mind and then follow the player around to several cities and stay with them for a period of time. Today, the process is very sophisticated with Central Scouting, computers, and new technology. Books are literally created on the good players and by the time every season begins, everyone knows who the best young players are. The really good ones are identified by the time they are 14 or 15 years old.

Nowadays, the real key is to try to find the hidden gems—the players who others don't know anything about at all. Finding the player who can play in the NHL that everyone else has missed is the key, and is very hard to do. Finding the All-Star player who is picked low in the draft is an important part of drafting, and that's been the key to Detroit's success in past 15 years.

There are meetings throughout the year. Lists of players are sent in by the scouts to the head scout, who completes the lists and puts everything in order. At the end of the year, meetings are held to put the drafting list of players together.

There was a time when it cost a team $1,000 to draft a player. Most teams didn't want to waste money and therefore wound up with just eight to 10 players. I recall when Emile Francis of the New York Rangers was drafting alone at the end of the day. He just kept picking players and paying the $1,000 for each one, looking for a hidden gem. Emile was a workaholic and he loved the game.

My philosophy in drafting was similar to others'. No matter how low a player was picked in the draft, never count him out. If you thought enough to pick the player, he must have some ability. You never know for sure when a young player will get bigger or faster or when he may mature and really develop as a player. My friend Phil Esposito was that way—and he became one of the greatest goal scorers to ever play the game.

When we drafted college players, I always encouraged them to stay in college and play for their school. I figured when they finished they would be available to us with a great deal of experience and would be farther along in their development skills. Occasionally the best ones might come out a year or so early, but most of the time it benefits the team and player to stay in school.

The one important thing that was always on the mind of the general manager is the budget. Most owners want the budget to balance and don't give free rein to spend at will. At some of our meetings I would have to explain to them our timing variances. "Why was our equipment and sticks budget out of line?" they'd ask. "Why were we spending X amount on travel?" I had to explain things about the building and about other things that we did. Unlike many teams, we were an extremely business-focused operation. I learned a great deal from the Gund brothers and it is one of the reasons that I have success in my business today.

"It was a slow day at the office for me if Louie didn't call me at least three times. He always started every conversation with, 'What are you going to give me today? You have to give me something!'"

—Bill Torrey, former general manager, New York Islanders

I watched every penny we spent, and I was always within budget. One year I wanted to spend $15,000 to remodel my office, and we didn't budget the money to do it. I wanted to fix it up in November but knew the money wasn't there. Therefore, I traded Kevin Maxwell for another player and got $15,000 cash as part of the deal. It allowed me to fix the office and not go over budget. So I called it my "Kevin Maxwell office."

One common thread that successful general managers possess is their business acumen. They have excellent business sense and would be successful in other arenas. People like Sam Pollock, Bill Torrey, Harry Sinden, Cliff Fletcher, Glen Sather, Bob Pulford, and others are all sound business leaders who could make a success of any other endeavor.

During the season, I was usually at work by 8:30 AM. I would immediately start checking around the league to see what was going on, who won the night before and who lost. Which players had played well and which had not. I checked for injuries and called other general managers to see what was going on in their world. I checked on player transactions to make sure that I was on top of any developments; I wanted to know of any player movement. I was obsessed with being up to date on everything.

Leading up to the draft, I might sit in the lobby of a hotel until 3:00 in the morning just to be sure I knew what was going on with other teams. I wanted to know which general managers were talking to each other. They used to think I was nuts staying up so late but I didn't want to miss one thing. I wanted to be in tune with what was happening and if I knew a deal was going down in my division that was going to really help one of the teams, I might have to find a way to sabotage the deal. The cat-and-mouse game never stopped for me.

Most days when I was at the office, I would eat lunch in the cafeteria. I rarely left the building. I would talk to the players, the coaches, and the trainer to keep up to date on what was happening with our team. If any of our scouts were around, I would talk to them to find out what they were doing, what players they had seen and where they were going.

I looked at the budget every day to be sure it was in line and I spent a lot of time on league issues as well. I was on a number of league committees that also required a great deal of my time.

I was on the rules committee, and was the chair of the Central League general managers for a couple of years. I was on the marketing committee; I served a stint as chair of the NHL general managers for a few years; Bill Torrey and I also served on the collective bargaining committee from 1978 to 1990. There were numerous others. This kept me traveling a significant amount on top of everything else that I had going.

I could handle all the work without much difficulty. I do it today with a vast amount of responsibility. It was the constant worry about winning that I couldn't handle. I enjoyed the competition. I liked my association with all of the other teams and general managers. I thrived on the action. The workload was never the problem. But the thought of not doing enough so we could win haunted me.

It was the obsessive-compulsive behavior that took over everything—especially on the days that we had games. The long days waiting for the game were very hard on me. During the game I would usually sit in the press box with the assistant coaches. If the game was going well and someone came by to see me, I would make them leave. I couldn't take the chance that their presence close to me might alter things. I would scream and yell, be angry, happy...I'd go through a tremendous spectrum of emotions during a game.

Losing, of course, was the worst of all. And it was especially bad if the loss was a fluke. There can be some very significant differences in losses. When we lost to Chicago in the playoffs in 1983, we outplayed them badly, but Murray Bannerman in the nets for Chicago beat us. It never should have happened, and to this day, I'm not over it.

Once we lost to St. Louis in a playoff game because of an official's bad call. We were short-handed and leading St. Louis when a penalty should have been called on them. The ref missed it and 10 seconds later put us two men down. They scored to tie the game and eventually won it. It was devastating and something over which we had no control. Those kinds of things were always the toughest to handle for me.

As I closed in on a decade at the job, things were getting really bad for me. I had just had enough. I was not taking any pills and the pressures were mounting by the day. I was trying my best to suffer through. I wasn't having any fun. In fact, I was becoming a basket case.

Fortunately for me and my family, I was able to leave most of those problems at work. I was also able to shield the players and staff with whom I worked every day. Basically, I was just doing it all to myself. And as bad as it was for me, it was still getting worse. The team was going through a terrible stretch and we had a massive number of injuries. Noel Rahn's offer was becoming more and more attractive by the minute.

I traveled to Montreal and I went to a game to look at some players with Gump Worsley. Gump was scouting for the team as well as working as the goalie coach. Gump's real name was Lorne John Worsley. He got his nickname because some of his friends thought he looked like the comic strip character Andy Gump. And the name stuck. Most people who knew him didn't even know it wasn't his real name. Gump was a great goalie who played for the Rangers and the Canadiens before finishing his career with the North Stars. He was also an outstanding goalie coach for us after he crossed over.

He asked me to go with him to scout a game up in Laval, Quebec. I remember it was very cold out in late January, and there was a lot of snow. We couldn't find a place to park, so we had to walk about three blocks in the deep snow to the arena. There were only 400 or so people at the game and I was cold and wet. It seemed like every person in the arena was smoking and sitting right on top of us. It was a horrible evening.

I thought to myself, *What am I doing here? I'm cold and wet, full of smoke, and completely miserable.* In the second period, I turned to Gump and said, "Hey Gump, let's go." He looked at me in absolute amazement and said, "What did you say? Are you sick? All the years that I have known you, you have never left a game early. What is wrong with you?"

I told him, "I just have a lot on my mind. Let's go." So we left. I had never done anything like that before, but it was too much. I didn't want to be there. It used to be that I could never get enough of hockey. That's what Gump remembered. But I wasn't the same. I was in trouble.

I went back to the hotel and thought about how I was not enjoying any of the things I was doing. I began asking myself, *Do I really want to be doing this any longer? How much more can I take?* I can still see myself sitting in that arena being about as miserable as I had ever been in my life.

A short time later, the team was playing a game in Hartford against the Whalers on a Saturday night. At the same time, Edmonton was playing the New York Islanders on the Island. The North Stars were scheduled for a game the following night in Philadelphia, and then home to play Edmonton on the following Wednesday. I told Glen Sonmor that I was going to scout the game in New York and that I would see him in Philadelphia on Sunday. I called my friend Bill Torrey, the Islanders general manager and told him I was coming to his game against the Oilers. He told me to meet him at the game and sit with him. His friend Gary Rice was there with him, and we all sat in his suite and watched the game.

My mind, however, was not on the Islanders game. It was on the scoreboard, on the score of our game against Hartford. Soon after it started, it was 1–0 Harford. Then it was 2–0 Hartford. It was killing me. I finally said to Bill, "I can't stand to watch that scoreboard. Give me your office keys. I'm going down to your office and I'll watch our game on television." So I went downstairs to Bill's office and soon we were behind 5–0 and playing terribly. I was really upset. I hated what was going on.

There I was in New York with my friend Bill Torrey, supposedly scouting and enjoying his game with him and his friend, and where was I? Sitting in his office alone, watching the North Stars get killed and dying a slow death.

The Islanders game ended and Bill came down to his office to invite me to go out with them for some drinks. I went along for about two seconds to a bar before I told Bill, "I have to get a cab and get back to the hotel. I'm going home."

Bill knew that I was really upset over our loss and I remember he said to me, "Louie, now don't do anything crazy." I also recall that Bill's friend Gary had asked me before the game, "Lou, are you okay? You look terrible! Why don't you quit this and go into the financial business like me? You'll have a lot more fun." It was pure coincidence—he didn't know that I was contemplating it at the time—but it struck a chord.

I went back to the hotel and called Francine several times that night. She is my best friend in the world and always helps me though everything. I told her that I was going to quit. I said that I would call owner Gordon Gund in the morning and go down to see him. It was time. I'd had enough. I told her that this time, absolutely, for sure, I was going to quit.

Gund lived in Princeton, New Jersey, and the train from New York to Philadelphia went directly through Princeton. So I called Gordon early the next morning and told him that I was coming to see him.

After talking to Gordon, I called Bill Torrey to tell him something very important. It related to an event that had occurred at our last GM meeting. Everyone had been complaining about their jobs. It seemed like everyone was getting in on it. And, as usual, there were myriad reasons why people thought we had a terrible job.

So I said to everyone, "You know, I have been sitting here listening to all of this complaining for the last 10 years and none of you ever do anything about it."

One of them said to me, "Well, Louie, you complain too, and you never do anything about it either."

"Yeah," I said, "but I'm going to quit. I'll be out of here before all of you guys will."

With my statement, Phil Esposito piped in and said, "Not before me. I'm going to quit before you do!"

I looked at him and said, "Name the stakes."

So we made a bet. Whoever quit first would win dinner for two at the restaurant of his choice and the most expensive wine on the menu. And Thayer Tutt wouldn't be paying for this meal!

So my call to Bill Torrey was very important. I said, "Listen, Bill, remember at our general managers meeting last January when Phil Esposito and I made a bet as to who would quit first? Well, I am going to quit today, but because the North Stars are on the road, the official announcement of my resignation will not be made until the team is back home. We play Wednesday so I will have a press conference on Thursday. If Phil Esposito quits between now and Thursday, you are my witness that I quit first and I won the bet!"

Torrey was floored. Of course, he couldn't care less about the bet. He said to me, "Louie, I told you not to do anything crazy!" I said to him, "It's not crazy. I should have done this a long time ago."

So right in the middle of one of the most important decisions of my career, which was to resign my position as general manager of the

Minnesota North Stars, I found it necessary to call Bill Torrey and solidify my position on my wager. I know it sounds nuts, but I like to win at everything I do—and I certainly was not going to lose that bet to Esposito!

The next day I met Gordon Gund to tender my resignation. I told him that I would stay until he found someone else but that I was definitely leaving, and that I would not stay past the upcoming player draft. I was considering accepting the job that Noel Rahn had been offering me for some time in money management.

Gordon is a great person as is his brother, George. They were wonderful owners and I was very fortunate to have had the opportunity to work for them. In addition to the North Stars, the Gunds have also owned the Cleveland Cavaliers of the NBA and have also owned the California Golden Seals, Cleveland Barons, and the San Jose Sharks of the National Hockey League. My primary contact was with Gordon, and we have a special relationship that continues to this day. He is a wonderful person, a terrific friend, and an outstanding mentor.

> *"I don't know anyone who doesn't like Lou Nanne. He has extraordinary energy and tremendous integrity. We were much more than just a business relationship. We were great friends."*
> —GORDON GUND, FORMER OWNER, MINNESOTA NORTH STARS

Once I told him my plans he immediately tried to talk me out of it. He countered by offering me the post of team president instead. He said they had planned to make a change there and that the job would be perfect for me. He encouraged me to think it over and to take Francine and go away for a week anywhere in the world at his expense. He really wanted me to stay with the team.

I asked a few preliminary questions about the presidency. Do I have to attend all the games? *No.* Do I have to worry about the wins and losses? *No.* Could I come to games, sit with the crowd, and have a drink? *Yes.* It sounded pretty good to me, but I had to think about it and talk to Francine.

He told me I would be in charge of the team's overall budget and that my responsibility would be to run the club like the business that it was. Then he said to me, "Now, take that trip and think it over. And stay away for a week!"

Our trip turned out to be more hectic than expected due to problems in the organization, but the new opportunity worked out for me and for the most part alleviated the stress I had endured in the general manager position. It was a very tough time for me and I needed the change badly.

When I finally called it quits after 10 years, I had 10 general managers call me and tell me they wished they could resign like I had. There was that much pressure on the job. For most of them, they had no other opportunities or alternatives. Some could not leave the competition. For others, it was their life.

As a general manager of a professional hockey team, the pressure is tremendous day in and day out. Mistakes are something that you must avoid. You had to make sure you drafted the right players, make sure you made the right trades, signed the right kind of contracts, and above all else in the process, win! You had to win. It was the ultimate goal. And when you did win, it was the highest of highs, and when you lost, it became the lowest of lows.

In today's game with the money involved, a mistake with a player could cost an organization as much as $50 million dollars. In our day, a mistake with a player might hit you for $250,000. Today a mistake of that magnitude could cripple an organization for years. If you wanted to do the job as a career, you had better not make too many of those mistakes.

Most of the pressure that comes with the job is internal, the pressure that you put on yourself. Many players and athletes are like me.

We hate to lose at anything we do. I don't care what I am doing—I want to win. If I am playing checkers with one of my grandkids, I want to win. It's me. It's just the way I am and I can't do anything about it.

Francine won't let me play volleyball with friends anymore, because even in a game like that I have to win and would slam a ball in someone's face to do it. I get too competitive and much too aggressive in any kind of competition, so I don't play anymore. If I find a sport or game that I am not very good at it, I don't want to play. It would be no fun for me if I lost or wasn't very adept at it. So I tend to stay away from those things.

There is one sport that I can play and not be crippled by my own competitiveness, and that is golf. I absolutely love to play, and don't get too mired in the competition of it. Don't get me wrong, I want to beat my friends and want to have a good score, but it doesn't bother me like other things do, if everything doesn't come out to perfection. And I suppose for me that is a good thing, because golf is one sport that could drive you nuts. My biggest goal in playing golf is to play quickly and enjoy my surroundings. I love playing on all the different courses.

But with just about everything else, the competitive drive will be there for me. Softball, baseball, basketball—it's all there. I'll run through people, knock them over, and do whatever it takes to win, even if it's just a game among family or friends.

Having this incredible passion for winning does not just come to you one day, it is a part of you, a part of your very being. I have always been that way. I have always wished I was as good at what I do on the first day as I become on the last day, because I would be so much better at it. If I had known as much the first day I was the general manager of the North Stars as I did the last day on the job, I would have been much more skilled and proficient, and I would have won much more. Unfortunately, life doesn't work that way.

I deeply appreciated what the Gunds did for me when I finally could not take it any longer. It was good for me at the time because it kept me involved with the game and the team I loved, but without the day-to-day pressures. But once they sold the team, that all changed. By then it was time for me to leave permanently. When Howard Baldwin took over and asked me to stay, I told him I would but we had to renegotiate my contract for one more year. He did, and I agreed to stay until the season was over. A few months later, Norm Green bought Howard out and I knew that I had made the right decision. Two years later, Norm moved the team to Dallas.

Although I cannot find significant fault in Norm's decision—he was losing a fortune, after all—it was devastating for the state, the region, and the Twin Cities, not to mention me personally. The North Stars were my team. I had been there since their infancy and had given them every single ounce of my energy for 23 years. I could not imagine the Twin Cities not having the North Stars. I just could not comprehend such a thing happening. But it did.

Norm tried hard to save the franchise. He put a small fortune into the Met Center in improvements and worked hard to try to find revenue to keep the team afloat. Norm was a real estate developer. He knew the business and he wanted to build a connecting shopping center from the Met Center to the Mall of America. He was turned down by the City of Bloomington. He went to the Metropolitan Facilities Commission and asked for more money for improvements for the Met Center. He was turned down.

Behind the scenes there was activity to get him to move to the Target Center to eliminate competition for that building. Norm was trying to make it work, but he couldn't do it, and he was forced to move the team. It was a very sad situation.

Even though the team was playing well at the time, he didn't have a large enough revenue stream. When the opportunity came for him to move the team to Dallas, he took it. As much as I love the Minnesota Wild, it is still difficult to see that there is not a Minnesota North Stars team here.

People often ask if I miss being involved with a pro hockey team. I don't miss any aspect of my role in hockey management. I had had enough. Like every other former player, I do miss playing. It was so much fun and I enjoyed every minute of it. I still wish I could lace up a pair of skates and go out and play today. It is a little bit hard for me to square that I got paid to play a game that I love. Could there be a better job?

I have been very fortunate to have the opportunity to participate in a sport that I dearly love. I haven't been able to play for a few years because of my new knee. I do get excited thinking about putting on a pair of skates and going to an outside rink. I love the game, but today I have the best of all worlds. I get to see quite a few games, and I don't have to go through my obsessions to enjoy them.

I am really enjoying the game again. As a fan, I go to the Wild games whenever I'm in the Twin Cities. I also go to the Gopher games, and I get to see my grandchildren play their games as well. I enjoy those games the most.

I read all the time to keep up with professional hockey and college hockey. I do a hockey radio show with Dan Barreiro on KFAN and this year I did the color commentary for my 46th Minnesota State Boys High School Hockey Tournament. My grandson's team, the Edina Hornets, won the championship. It was a tremendous thrill to broadcast those games. But I will say, they were the toughest I've ever had to do. It was a very unique experience watching my grandson Louie play for the championship, just as his father, Marty, had in 1984.

Since I put the business behind me, I have awakened on two occasions from a sound sleep in a cold sweat. Both times I was back in the game, a general manager again. When I realized it was only a nightmare, I felt a tremendous sense of relief wash over me.

That said, I truly wish I was still playing today—I love the game that much. But the journey is over and I now can enjoy the game without feeling that winning is everything.

Although I will say when I am watching a game, and my grand-son's team is ahead, I might just have to keep my hands in my pocket a certain way. After all, "I reserve the right to revert."

5

Obsessions, Compulsions, and Superstitions

It was a huge playoff game for us. We should have won the game; we had lots of chances. Usually when we played a game that well, we won. But not on that night. I tried everything possible to win it. I walked around the chair this way, and then I walked around the chair that way. I sat a certain way and in a certain place in the press box. I went downstairs, back to the press box, and then downstairs again. If it helped that I not watch the game, then I didn't watch. I'd sit at my desk and hold the desk a certain way. I was doing all kinds of crazy things that night, making every effort that I could to win the game. None of it worked. Despite all of my actions, we still lost.

I think I have a good grasp of all of the things that I do and have done through the years to help my teams win games. I understand it, and I acknowledge that it is crazy stuff that could not possibly make a difference in the outcome of a game. Yet I do it anyway.

The definition from the Mayo Clinic (www.mayoclinic.com) of obsessive-compulsive disorder is in part:

> A type of anxiety disorder in which you have unreasonable thoughts and fears (obsessions) that lead you to engage in repetitive behaviors (compulsions). With obsessive-compulsive disorder, you may realize that your obsessions aren't reasonable, and you may try to ignore them or stop them. But that only increases your distress and anxiety. Ultimately, you feel driven to perform compulsive acts in an effort to ease your distress.

Most of my behaviors set my mind right and allow me to do what I have to do, or be able to watch what I am going to watch. That's different from superstitions. I think that obsessive behavior is a heightened degree of superstition.

Many athletes have superstitions. Phil Esposito and the crossed sticks in the locker room comes to mind. Some players have to put their skates on the same way and dress in a certain order. My obsessions got worse as the competitive levels that I was involved in increased. Once I quit the job of general manager, the obsession for the winning games went out of my daily routine. I got better, and today I am much better. However, as I told my wife, I reserve the right to revert. With this in mind, I always know that my comfort level is only a few quirks away.

But the quirky behavior certainly doesn't stop with sports. It is a serious disorder that affects many people in many different ways. I really never thought about the fact that I had OCD until I appeared on *The Oprah Winfrey Show* and listened to their discussions of odd behavior.

OCD affects everyone differently. It has affected me in many different ways. I would have to do things a certain way in order for my mind to feel right about it. It was a way to settle my mind and move on to what I had to do next. When I was 16, I drove up my driveway in a downpour as I listened to the Detroit Tigers on the radio. My younger brother Mike ran out of the house and tried to open the car door. It was locked and he asked me to open it so he could get out of the rain. I told him I couldn't because Detroit was leading the Yanks in the bottom of the ninth and I was afraid he would jinx them. I can still picture him screaming at me with rain running down his face. But I had to make sure Detroit won.

The things I have done over the years are countless. They existed for the most part because of success. I would re-create in my own mind what worked before and I had to do it again and in the same manner to get the same results.

The dress, the skates, the shin pads, how high I cut my stick, how I taped the knob of my stick, the blade on my stick—all those things and many more became a part of what I did. They just continued to grow. And then if something did not come about the way I wanted it to and we lost a game, I would naturally change things. It was endless. On numerous occasions as GM, I would have the team change hotels if we had lost in that city on the previous trip.

When I was playing for the North Stars, my teammates would make fun of me because they knew what I was doing. They could see what was going on. For example, they knew that I always had to follow Bill Goldsworthy out of the locker room, so they would try to mess that up for me. I would actually have to hide behind doors to make sure that "Goldy" did not sneak out of the locker room before me. I *had* to follow him out to the ice.

I would never tie my skates until Murray Oliver tied his first. So he too would play games with me. He would bend over to tie his skates, stop, and then straighten up. Then he would go back down again to tie his skates. He had a blast with me and tried to throw me off course, and it drove me nuts. My good friend and old roommate Tom Reid used to toy with me constantly.

Naturally, this didn't stay in the locker room. Reporters would hear about it and write about it. The topic of obsessions and compulsions made for a good story. Many people go through this in their daily lives and they don't realize that what they're doing is OCD. The basketball coach who appeared on *Oprah* with me had the same problem but was in denial.

They also had a man on the show who had the obsession to straighten the shelves in grocery stores, and a woman who, if she left her house, would not return for four days. She would live in her car and clean up at the YMCA. There was another woman who washed herself so thoroughly that her skin would bleed. Then we all ended up on the same program, intended to make people aware of obsessive-compulsive behavior and how difficult it can be when it takes over your life. I was able to recognize the problem very clearly from that point on.

"Lou went to check an opponent in one of our games and instead cross-checked me in the face, which cost me 13 teeth! But I have forgiven him. How could you not forgive Lou Nanne?"

—TOM REID, FORMER
NORTH STARS TEAMMATE

When competition arises, I do revert. If I am going to make a sales presentation, I might want to wear a certain suit. Now, that sounds all right on the surface. Someone might want to wear their best suit or their best color; that's pretty common. I wear mine because I feel it is a good omen. I may have worn it when we previously got a new account, or I may be wearing it because another didn't work at an earlier meeting.

I might hand out the presentation materials left to right rather than right to left. I might have to introduce people in a certain manner. I will insert certain phrases in my presentation because they were successful. I realize it will not make the presentation better, but if my mind is comfortable and I feel we will be a success.

118

Those of us who are aware of the disorder realize these quirks have no effect on the outcome. But we feel better and definitely have more composure as well as more confidence in the outcome. In my mind it helps, even though I know it is a total waste of energy. By doing these things I know that I am using energy without benefit from it.

I might be sitting at home watching the Wild play on television and the other team scores a goal. I will change the channel because the opponent scored and then go back to watching the game. Obviously, switching the channel has absolutely nothing to do with the game but I make the change thinking it will help the Wild. I know it is ridiculous. I really do, but I do it anyway.

It drives Francine nuts because she knows I am going to do it, but I can't help it. I just have to do it. Believe me, I know how crazy it is. I will be sitting at home, changing the channel on my television set thinking that it is going to help the Wild in Montreal. I will do it and feel good about it.

Some things, though, make me uncomfortable. For instance, if I am watching a game on television and I have my hands on the table a certain way and we score, I might leave my hands in the same place for the rest of the game. I cannot move my hands. I just cannot do it. My hands will stay on that table in that position for the rest of the game. I might leave my hands in the same place for three periods knowing it will not affect the game in any way.

One night we had some friends, Pete Karos and his wife, Artie, over to our house for dinner. The team was playing in Toronto and we were leading 3–2 with about four minutes left in the game. I didn't make the road trip with the team and we were all sitting in the living room watching it.

All of a sudden Pete stands up. I look over at him and say, "Pete, where are you going?" He says, "I have to use the bathroom." I tell him, "Pete, sit down." He says, "No Lou, seriously I need to use the bathroom." "Pete, sit down! You are not going to use the bathroom. If I have to get up, grab you, and throw you down I will, because you are not going to use the bathroom. You are going to have to wait until this game is over. We are ahead 3–2 and you cannot move! Look at me, my hands haven't left the chair handles."

He says to me, "Lou, I am going to wet my pants then." I tell him, "Pete, that's okay, wet your pants. Go right in your pants right there, because you are not moving." He looks right at me and says "You are crazy!" And I said back to him, "Yes I am, but you are not moving!"

It was that way with me. In my mind, if he moved, they might score and we would lose the game.

This obsession knows no bounds. During a Montreal game, George Gund came over to talk to me. As soon as he got there, the Canadiens had a great chance to score and barely missed getting a goal. I said to him, "George, you are going to have to leave the area." He looked at me and said, "What do you mean?" I said, "George, bad luck could come from you standing here. You have to leave. I will talk to you later." Let's just say, I'm happy he didn't fire me. Behavior like that is obsessive-compulsive at its worst.

The biggest thing today is that I know what it is and the key is I am comfortable with it. That is in itself a huge part of the battle. I know what I do is quirky and I know it's is crazy but I am fine with it because it makes my mind relaxed. It gives me mental calmness. The mental calmness is really important to me when I am in a competition. I hope others can learn from this and it can help them deal with their issues. The most important thing for anyone who is OCD is to recognize it in himself or herself, and to get treatment for it.

Athletes have different ways of preparation, and the unusual ones stand out. Some people like to sleep; some want to walk around. I had to get all my things in order before the game started and then I was ready to play. For example, when we came down for warm-ups before the game, I would go around the net two times to the right and then twice to the left. First I would take a slap shot and then go around the net twice, right to left, and then take a wrist shot and go around the net twice, left to right. When the game began, everyone on the bench knew what I was going to do. I would come off the ice, take a drink, spit it out, then take a drink and swallow it. Then take another drink and spit it out and take another drink and swallow it. I had to do that four times total. And then I would take a piece of ice and suck it down and then take another piece of ice and spit it out.

I was asked once what would have happened if by chance Goldsworthy had gone out on the ice before me. My answer was, "I would follow someone with the same initials or closest to them."

If you cannot get comfortable with your particular issues, no matter how bizarre they may be, then you should seek medical attention. But whatever it is you end up doing, you have to be comfortable with it. I have accepted it and I am comfortable with it. In addition, I think those that suffer from this disorder need to fully understand it. Once you understand it, then you have to analyze what kind of effect it is having on you as a person. Is it affecting you, your work, your health, your family? My family understands it and expects it from me. It is who I am but I have control of it enough that I don't let it affect my work or family. I envy people who don't have OCD. They are fortunate that they don't have to expend so much energy in such a useless way.

I don't think my obsessions will ever get as bad as they were when I was GM, but they are still with me. I mentioned the need to revert during sales presentations, and they are also prevalent when I am watching my grandkids play their games.

People I know are often amazed that I am willing to talk about my condition for fear of what others might think of me. It doesn't bother me because I know I have to face these idiosyncrasies myself. It is something that I have to do, pure and simple. I am not afraid to talk about the issue. Everyone has to face situations that may trouble them, but we all have to resolve them to the best of our ability.

By discussing OCD, I hope I will help others in the process. I understand what my issues are and I know what I am doing will have absolutely no effect on the outcome of anything that I am trying to influence. I am not embarrassed to talk about it. Why should I be?

6

My Greats of the Past and Present

He is called simply "the Great One." This is different than people recognizing a first name, like Mickey or Willie in baseball, Peyton and Fran in football, the Phil and Tiger of golf, or the Wilt and Magic of basketball.

These three words strung together simply signify the best ever. It doesn't even define a particular sport. It stands alone: the Great One. And the label is that it is universally claimed by him; no other sports have their great one. And without question, everyone knows exactly who that great one is. There have been few athletes with distinctive titles like this one, and none more apt than the moniker for Wayne Gretzky.

I have been very fortunate through my playing career and in my years in management to become friends with great athletes and great people. One of them is Wayne Gretzky.

Whenever I watched him play I would wonder, *How can anyone be this good?* He possessed something that all of the greats had: the ability to "play the game from the press box." Average players in hockey play the game at ice level and at its furious pace, seemingly 100 miles an hour. The greats of the game, like Gretzky, seem to play the game from the press box, meaning their game evolves at a much slower speed, giving them more time to make plays and score goals.

The superstars of the game operate in what we call elongated time. We say they waltz while the rest jitterbug. They know where to go before the rest of us do. Instead of going to where the puck was at any given moment, Gretzky would go to where the puck would be headed—before it was even sent. He had the ability to foresee what was going to occur on the ice. You can bet that all the great athletes have the advantage of playing with elongated time.

When I first took over the North Stars, I hired a research firm in Nebraska to help us identify the best players to draft. The firm developed a test to help us select players who excelled with the concept of elongated time, or anticipatory thinking. Gretzky was simply on a plane above everyone else. You could compile a list of all of the unbelievable skills of the greatest players in the world; Gretzky had them all. He was remarkable!

Bobby Orr was another. As a matter of fact, at a general managers' meeting in Florida, 12 of us were sitting around discussing what player—of all time—we would want to build a team around. Six picked Gretzky and six picked Orr.

Ted Williams said that he used to be able to see the stitching on a baseball as it came toward him at 90-plus miles per hour. Anyone who was ever great in their sport would say that the game seemingly slowed down for them and that's why they became so proficient at their trade. Look at Joe Mauer of the Minnesota Twins. It seems like he waits forever on a pitch before swinging, and then he drives the ball out to left field.

I remember our outstanding goalie Cesare Maniago, after a game in the Boston Garden, griping about how frustrated he was that Phil

Esposito had scored on him *again*. I recall him saying to me, "Louie, I can't take it anymore. I am so upset at Esposito and the time he takes to shoot. He gets the puck in front of the net and I know he is going to try to put it in. It seems he has only has a split-second to shoot. So I wait and I wait and I wait before I move. And then finally, when I don't think I can wait another second, I make my move. But he always has the ability to wait longer. And as soon as I move, he shoots to wherever I have moved from and scores."

Phil had that tremendous feel for the game. And when he was in front of the net with the puck, he could wait until the very last split second and then put the puck in the spot that the goalie had just vacated. This ability is something that can't be learned or developed; it is innate to only the best.

When I became general manager of the North Stars in 1978, we had finished in last place in the previous season and had first pick in the draft. I went through our scouting lists and the Central Scouting lists; all of them had Bobby Smith rated as the No. 1 player. Still, I wanted to take a look at Bobby Smith before the draft. He was playing for Ottawa at the time, so I went to my hometown, Sault Ste. Marie, where his Ottawa team was facing off against the Greyhounds.

My cousin said to me before the game, "Now, Louie, listen to me. There is a kid that is going to be playing tonight that you will barely notice in the game. But when the game is over you are going to find that he has three or four points. He does it every single night." I said to him, "Who is it?" He said, "His name is Wayne Gretzky." Sure enough, when the game was over, the three stars selected for the game were Gretzky, Craig Hartsburg, and Bobby Smith.

That was the first time I ever saw Gretzky play and he finished the night with three points. You barely noticed him on the ice. He was a very small, frail kid at the time, compared to Bobby Smith who was a big, dominant player.

Another good player in that same game was Steve Payne, who went on to have a good career with Minnesota. I eventually wound up getting Smith, Craig Hartsburg, and Payne to play for the North Stars. At the time, Gretzky was not available because he was only 16 years old but he kept getting those points night after night and filling hockey rinks all over Ontario.

The next year Gretzky signed with the World Hockey Association (WHA) and went to play for Indianapolis in the new league at 17. At the time we had the rights to the Indianapolis goaltender, Eddie Mio. So one night I went to watch Indianapolis play and ran into Glen Sather at the game. Glen was the general manager of Edmonton in the WHA. Gretzky got three goals in the game, his first hat trick in professional hockey.

Glen told me that he had heard that the Indianapolis owner was entertaining the idea of selling Wayne Gretzky's rights to Edmonton to settle a debt. Needless to say, Edmonton made the deal and a dynasty was about to begin.

Some years later I was with Barry Shenkarow, owner of the Winnipeg Jets, and told him the Gretzky story. He told me he had been offered the same deal by Indianapolis to buy Gretzky. He said to me, "Louie, I went to our general manager, Rudy Pilous, with the same deal opportunity and asked him what he thought. Rudy said to me, 'The kid is too small and he will never play in the National Hockey League.' So we didn't take the offer." Unfortunately having the opportunity to get Wayne Gretzky and passing probably cost them the Stanley Cup. But then it's always difficult to project 17-year-olds.

I attended a board of governors meeting when the merger of the NHL and four WHA teams was under consideration. I was asked by Bill Wirtz of Chicago to meet several of the team owners on his boat at 11:00 that night. There were 11 owners there and Bill asked me to design a plan that would satisfy them all.

So I went around to each person and asked them what they wanted out of the merger. Some wanted players on their draft list, some wanted players from the folded WHA teams, and others wanted draft choices. We put together a system that essentially made everyone happy in the room. We needed all 11 votes to carry the merger through.

The most unusual request concerned Wayne Gretzky. Vancouver Canucks owner Frank Griffith insisted that Gretzky remain in Edmonton. His representative for the Canucks organization said this was paramount; he wouldn't support the deal otherwise. That was extremely kind of Frank and obviously very important to Edmonton even though Gretzky was going to be 18 and ineligible for the NHL draft that year.

The next year, the All-Star Game was in Detroit and I was able to get a couple of tickets for Gretzky's parents who had come in at the last minute for the game. They sat with my wife and me at the game and have never forgotten it. Whenever I run into Wayne's dad, he tells people that I got him tickets to his first All-Star Game. They are very appreciative people and wonderful individuals, just like Wayne.

Wayne Gretzky handled the puck on the ice like a magician. He was so creative and watching him perform was beyond comprehension—he was that good. His hand skills were phenomenal, his peripheral vision was incredible, and he had an amazing perception of what was happening during the game. As said before and often by broadcasters of his games, "Most players go to where the puck is. Gretzky goes to where the puck is going to come."

He had incredible quickness, tremendous skating agility, and just uncanny skills. The talent that Wayne demonstrated on the ice night after night comes along once in a lifetime. If you spent enough time watching Gretzky play, you would be mesmerized. He would come up with something new every time he went on the ice. He did things with the puck that had never been seen before or since. While other players spun and chased and skated, Gretzky operated like a ballet dancer, with grace and precision. Anyone who ever had the opportunity to see him play should consider himself very fortunate.

Gretzky played in the National Hockey League from 1979 to 1999 and during that time period, he became the greatest hockey player of all time. He became "the Great One."

Another player of incredible ability who became the greatest defenseman to play the game was the incomparable Bobby Orr. Bobby, like Wayne, is an extremely kind person—and his playing skills also were unbelievable. I will never forget the introduction he gave me in my rookie season. I thought I had a clear lane up the middle to start a rush. As soon as I passed the puck, Bobby stopped, whirled, and intercepted it. He took one stride over our blue line and scored so fast with a slap shot that my head spun. I could hardly believe what had happened! He just simply took over hockey games and literally could not be stopped.

Bobby and Wayne were the best who ever played. One was a defenseman and the other was a forward, both with ability off the charts. They were in a league of their own and they made everyone around them better at their game.

I got to know Bobby through my lifelong friend and his Bruins teammate, Phil Esposito. Bobby would often come out with us after games and sometimes the day before we played each other. He is a marvelous person—a kind, caring, and thoughtful human being. On the ice he was electrifying and as dynamic as he could be, and off the ice he was quiet, reserved, and extremely generous.

After a game at the Met Center, I was leaving the building and a fan hollered at me, "Hey, Nanne, why don't you hit Bobby Orr?" I wanted to yell back at the guy, "I would like to, but I couldn't hit him if I threw a bucket of confetti at him." He was here one second and there the next.

Bobby was such a great player that I always thought it was just pure pleasure to watch him play the game. I have thought many times that there cannot be a greater thrill in hockey than to watch Gretzky and Orr play the game. Even when the opposing teams focused everything they had on containing them, it never worked. They were just that good.

I always found it incredible to watch the great superstars of the game; you would look at them play and know they were better than anyone else. And then you would watch Gretzky and Orr and know they were a level above the superstars.

Bobby Orr spent most of his career with the Boston Bruins, finishing his last two seasons with the Chicago Blackhawks. He is the greatest defenseman to ever playing the game. I simply can't imagine what he could have accomplished if injuries had not cut short his hockey career.

During the time that Bobby Orr played he was without a doubt the most feared player in all of hockey. He could beat you in so many ways. He could beat you with his playmaking, his stick handling, his skating, his shooting, his passing, and his uncanny ability take over a game. He was a phenomenal player.

I used to watch Bobby Orr on the ice and dream of what it must be like to be able to play the game like he did. When you were playing against him, it was easy to fall into the trap of watching him perform.

I recall someone once saying that Orr should have been a forward. I think he would have been misplaced there. Don't get me wrong, he could have been great at any position, but as a defenseman he controlled the game. He could see everything from back there and kept the game in his control. He was absolutely amazing.

Teams would literally try everything to stop Orr when they played the Bruins; few things ever worked. Scotty Bowman tried putting someone on Orr every second. He put a good checker on the ice just to sit on Orr. The strategy failed. No one could stay with him. Like Gretzky, I would watch him and wonder, *How can anyone be that good?* Some teams tried to keep the puck away from his side of the ice, but sure enough, he'd find a way to get it.

Another player I admired is Pittsburgh Penguins player Mario Lemieux. Mario had all the skills necessary to be a great player—and then on top of all that he had the incredible size to go with it. It was almost impossible to check him. He could keep his body between you and the puck and he might have the puck some eight feet from you. You absolutely could not get close to him. He was so big and so strong. He was just unbelievable. He had the superb hand skills that a hockey player needs to be successful, monstrous strength, and great speed. It didn't matter how good someone was defensively, it was extremely difficult to defend against him with his puck-handling skills and size.

I honestly think that Mario Lemieux became one of the four greatest players of all time after he played with Wayne Gretzky in the Canada Cup. After that game, he returned to his team and became a real leader and a dominant force in the National Hockey League. After winning the Cup, his passion was palpable.

Lemieux could do almost anything with the puck. He may have been the best stick handler of all time. Because of his size, tremendous strength, and hand skills, he could do some things on the ice that no one else could do. For a defenseman to look up and see Lemieux coming down the ice was a nightmare. There was a time that a defenseman could put his stick between the legs of a player in an attempt to immobilize the player. It is illegal to do that now. Failing that method, stopping Lemieux was impossible. It would be easier to stay home sick. Lemieux played his entire career with Pittsburgh and is now the owner and general partner.

In an earlier era in professional hockey, the three that stand apart from the others are: Gordie Howe, Maurice "Rocket" Richard, and Bobby Hull. Gordie Howe—especially when playing his early days with the Detroit Red Wings—was in a different era of professional hockey. He was bigger, faster, and stronger than most other players, and on the ice he was as mean as they come. I remember playing with him in a legends game. I asked Gordie to sign my jersey so I would have a souvenir. Pretty soon we had all the players signing everybody else's jerseys. Gordie thought that was just great and told his wife about it.

She said to me, "Louie, Gordie won't keep that jersey. You watch. He will give it to someone. I remember what he did when I bought him a painting of Joe DiMaggio at some fundraiser that we attended in Palm Springs. After the auction Gordie went up to Joe to have him sign the painting. Joe told him that it was the best likeness of himself that he had ever seen, and Gordie gave him the painting."

He was a very kind man—off the ice. On the ice, he would cut your head off with his stick if it meant the difference between winning and losing. There was no question about it, he played to win.

One night we were playing an exhibition game against the Red Wings and Wayne Connelly and I were sitting in the press box watching the game. (It was our turn to have a game off.) During the game, Howe came up the ice with the puck and Connelly said to me, "Look at that distance between Howe and all the other players. If our opponents stayed that far away from me, I would have scored 50 goals a year."

Just as Wayne finished saying it, Larry Hillman got close to Howe to check him, Howe hit him in the throat with his stick, and Larry was carried off the ice. I looked over at Connelly and said, "Now do you understand why no one gets close to Howe on the ice!"

Howe set the tone as "everyone's hockey player." He was big, strong, had a great shot, and was as tough as they come. He had a tremendous shot release and an incredible ability to read the play as it was happening. He could do it all. Lemieux was big and strong like Howe and was very good at holding you away, but Howe would just knock you away from the play.

When you played against Gordie Howe, you had better be careful, because he would find a way to hurt you. He would keep his elbow up and let you have a part of it if he had the chance. And if you tried to get to him, you likely would eat some wood. He would cut you with that stick as quick as he would look at you.

Gordie had the great honor and privilege in his career to do what few athletes ever have the chance to do. At the end of his career he played with his sons on the same team. Marty was good, and Mark was a special player. And no one messed with either of them while Gordie was around.

I loved to watch him play the game. He was my true hero growing up in the Soo. And he was a Red Wing, the closest team to my home and the best of the best. Howe seemed to play forever, having a career that spanned five decades. He started in 1946 and played until 1980.

Some people would make the argument—especially if they happened to live in Montreal—that the best of that era was "Rocket" Richard of the Canadiens. Richard was a terrific player also and I suppose that between the two, you could make a case for either one of them being the best. They were both great hockey players and inarguably the pair who dominated the game during their careers.

Richard was a tremendous goal scorer for the Canadiens and the face of hockey in Canada. It seemed like the Canadiens won the Stanley Cup in every year that Richard played, even though it wasn't quite that way. They did win it eight times during his career, and he was the captain of the team when they won four consecutive Cups from 1957 to 1960.

Like Howe, Richard was another player who would do anything to win. They were special players and especially tough when the chips were down. Richard was the most dangerous from the blue line in to the opposition net; his intensity there was unmatched.

Another tremendous player and favorite of the fans was the great Bobby Hull of the Chicago Blackhawks. Hull was flamboyant, powerful, and had the best slap shot the game had ever seen. He had tremendous energy and is a great ambassador for the game. He truly loved the game of hockey and he loved life.

Hull had everything you would want in a player and was a fantastic attraction. He had a bullet shot. He was just captivating to watch. He was powerfully built and had that wavy long blond hair.

At the time that he played there was no one else in all of sports who was more charismatic. When the Hawks were on the power play and Bobby would pick the puck up behind the net and start up the ice, it was as thrilling to watch as anything in any sport. He would skate around his opponents, cross the blue line, and let that booming shot fly. It was riveting, like nothing else you had ever seen before.

One night in Chicago he hit Gump Worsley in the face with one of his rocket shots. Gump was lucky to live; he didn't wear a mask. Apparently the puck turned and he was hit by the flat side of the puck instead the edge. That twist of fate probably saved his life.

Some years ago, a sports show did a program on the speed of Hull's slap shot. They followed the shot with a camera and focused on the goalie as well. They then slowed everything down into frames so you could watch the goalie react to the shot. It was amazing. You could see the shot go past the goalie and hit the net, and then the goalie would react after the puck was already by him.

Bobby was a matinee idol. He was a superhero. He could fly down the ice. He was colorful, strong, and fit his nickname, "the Golden Jet." After he hit Gump in the face that night in Chicago,

Gump did not want to face him again. In fact, when Gump was with the North Stars, Cesare would always play against the Blackhawks. It seemed that Gump would come down with the flu or mysteriously feel ill. Gump was smart. He wasn't going to get killed by Hull's shot.

When the World Hockey Association was formed, Bobby became the frontperson for the league. He gave it instant credibility. The Chicago franchise suffered for years after his departure.

Bobby was also a good guy. One night, he, Phil Esposito, and I were out to dinner and we started talking about some player. I said, "Yeah, but he doesn't like to get hit." Bobby looked over at me and said, "I don't like to get hit." And I thought about it after and I thought, "I don't like to get hit either." I had just never thought about it that way before. But it made perfect sense: why would anyone like to get hit? Although while thinking about that, I do remember one game where I was really sluggish and couldn't get myself into the game. I recall at the time thinking, *I wish someone would put a big check on me and wake me up.* Maybe some players like to be hit after all.

Having the great honor and good fortune to have watched these three greats play, and then to have played against Gordie and Bobby, remain among my greatest thrills. Howe, Richard, and Bobby Hull were some of the biggest names in all of sports, and they certainly earned their reputations.

Denis Potvin was another terrific player who played for the New York Islanders from 1973 to 1988. He was the first pick overall of the Islanders and remained with them his entire career. When Orr retired, Potvin was thought to be the premier defenseman in the game, along with Larry Robinson of Montreal.

Denis scored 30 goals in two consecutive seasons—as a defenseman. He could do everything on the ice. He was a great playmaker, tremendous with the puck, and had great vision on the ice. My friend Bill Torrey knew what he was doing when he drafted Potvin. Bill went on to build his great teams around him.

I also thought Doug Harvey was a tremendous player. He was another player who saw the game in slow motion. He was an unbelievable passer and puck handler. Doug knew the game and he knew how to move the puck up the ice and take control of the play.

I can still see Doug Harvey in my mind's eye. I can see him coming up the ice with the puck. He was phenomenal. But as good as Doug Harvey and Denis Potvin were as defensemen—better than most who played the game—Orr was at a different level.

I would also be greatly remiss if I didn't mention my close friend through most of my life, Phil Esposito. Phil was the highest scoring center of all time until Wayne Gretzky came along and surpassed him. Phil had an absolutely unbelievable release. He could pick spots like you would not believe and score from impossible locations.

I remember when he and his brother Tony ran their hockey camp in the Soo. I was there working with the kids for a week and I really enjoyed it. One day after practice, Tony asked Phil to stay and take some shots at the goalies. I still have a hard time believing what I saw him do that afternoon. The first goalie took his place in the net and Phil positioned himself about 20 feet from the goal and put 10 pucks down on the ice. The goalie was 18 years old and a big kid. He came out of the net to cut down the angle that Phil had to shoot at. Phil just shot at him without moving and with little if any room at all, he put nine of the 10 in the net. One after another he fired right to different spots. There was no room at all to put the puck past the goalie but Phil did it and made the kid look helpless.

When I had my hockey school in Richfield, Minnesota, Phil put on an exhibition of shooting one day that was practically otherworldly.

He was demonstrating how to hit a spot on the boards with the puck. Over and over again he hit the same spot on the boards. I recall J.P. Parise, who was one of the instructors, watching Phil. He turned to me and said, "Wow, do I ever have a lot of work to do!"

Phil Esposito was absolutely amazing and maybe the best man to ever play the game in front of the nets. With his incredible shooting ability, quick release, and elongated capability, it is a wonder that he didn't score every time he shot the puck.

I have been very fortunate in my hockey connections to meet some great people. They don't rise to the status of Gretzky, Orr, Lemieux, Howe, Richard, or Hull in hockey skills and ability, but they have other characteristics of their personal makeup that have always meant a lot to me through the years.

There were three players in my time that I always felt exuded class, presence, and were truly remarkable people. And although I had the opportunity to meet and get to know the best players, these three stood out for their dignity and I was honored to know them: Jean Beliveau, the great Montreal Canadien; Jean Ratelle; and the late Bill Masterton. They were similar in the way they carried themselves, and their grace garnered the respect of everyone who came in contact with them.

I believe there are things about certain people that just have a way of striking you. These three did that with me. They are very unique individuals.

Jean Beliveau was a true statesman. H was the classiest guy to ever play in the National Hockey League and one of the most dominant players to ever lace up a pair of skates. He was outstanding at distributing the puck, played smart, and had a dynamic style that made his presence memorable in every game he played. After he retired and began working as an ambassador for the Montreal Canadiens, Jean was asked to be the governor general of Canada. This is an appointed position, and one of extreme esteem. Put simply, one is not offered that kind of opportunity unless he is quite special. He turned it down. Sometime later I was with him and asked him why.

He told me, "Lou, when you represent Canada, you know that you have to go to a lot of parties and all kinds of events. I really don't like that kind of thing, so I turned it down. I have too many of them with Montreal, and I would have even more in that position."

That's Jean, a person with such an incredible amount of class and presence but also privacy. He always operated with a special sense of dignity and I have always admired that in him.

Jean was a great player. He played parts of 20 seasons with Montreal and was one of the best. He was on 10 Stanley Cup championship teams, and as an executive with the club, he was a part of seven more. He played in an incredible 1,125 games for Montreal, scored an amazing 507 goals and 712 assists, and was an All-Star 13 times.

Jean Ratelle was a wonderful player for the New York Rangers and the Boston Bruins. Like Beliveau, he is also a hockey hall of famer, though he never really got the recognition that some others did. He played in 1,281 NHL games and scored 491 goals with 776 assists. Like Beliveau, anyone around him felt in awe. His quiet yet powerful disposition and class is evident to everyone who meets him.

Bill Masterton was another of the finest people I have known. He had such a warm, caring, and wonderful personality—and the manner in which he carried himself was very special. He was a creative player who saw the ice very well. He was extremely intelligent and, although not the best of skaters, his intelligence and understanding of the game, in addition to his hand skills, more than made up for it.

I got to know him in our collegiate days when he played for the University of Denver. He was such a gifted, talented leader and an All-American at Denver. The team that he played on at Denver may have been the best collegiate hockey team ever put together. They were incredible and Bill was the best of them.

When Bill finished college, Murray Williamson got him a job at Honeywell and he played in United States Hockey League for the South St. Paul Steers. I was with Rochester at the time, so we got to play against each other again. When Murray Williamson arranged for Bill to get his U.S. citizenship, Bill and I spent one year on the U.S. National Team together. Bill then signed with the North Stars before the 1968 Olympics and I stayed with the Olympic Team.

At the time, there were three reasons why I didn't turn professional. First, I was in training for the Olympics and I had always wanted to be an Olympian. Once I had seen the 1960 team win the gold medal, I knew it would be a huge accomplishment to play in the Olympic Games. Second, I didn't feel that the offers that I was getting to turn professional were high enough, so I had no issue with waiting. Third, I was waiting for my citizenship to come through. I've always been glad I waited.

So I had the wonderful experience of playing with and against Bill Masterton. I was very pleased when I learned that he had scored the first goal ever in Minnesota North Stars history at the beginning of the 1967–68 season of play.

Only four minutes into the game on January 13, 1968, in a game between the North Stars and the Oakland Seals at the Met Center, Masterton was checked by two Seals players and fell backwards on to the ice, striking his head as he hit the surface. The results of the blow to his head caused a massive brain hemorrhage that resulted in his death two days later.

Bill's loss was a tragedy. The hockey world was devastated that one of the great people was taken from the world and from his wonderful family. His injury and subsequent death resulted in intense lobbying efforts for players to wear helmets. By 1979 they were mandated for players entering the NHL.

The night that Bill was injured, I was in Boston with the U.S. Olympic Team. We had just played Boston University and were leaving to go back to Minneapolis. At the same time, the North Stars crossed paths with us, taking a charter flight to Boston after their game in Minnesota. I remained in Boston because I was doing a North Stars scoreboard show for the team. After their games, I was also asked to do the color commentary for the North Stars game in Boston with local broadcaster Frank Buetel.

The team was delayed on their flight to Boston I sat there waiting for them to arrive. I had heard about Bill's injury and then I heard that he died. I was devastated. It was time to go on the air and the team had not arrived and I had to do the half hour pregame show alone. It was a tough night—one of the most difficult of my broadcasting career.

Jean Beliveau, Jean Ratelle, and Bill Masterton. I don't know of anyone that I ever met in all of sports that had the presence and class of these three.

Over a 23-year span in the National Hockey League I kept very little memorabilia. Today, I have only a few pictures of hockey players in my home. Gordie Howe is one of them, along with a few of my other hockey friends including Bobby Orr, Phil Esposito, and Wayne Gretzky; names of iconic magnitude in hockey fame. I feel fortunate and honored to have held their friendships for many years.

• • •

Earlier I mentioned that are three people who have had the biggest influence on my life: my father, John Mariucci, and Walter Bush.

I have already written at length about my father and Mariucci, but I would be greatly remiss if I did not mention Walter Bush here.

Walter has had such a positive effect on me through all the years that we have known each other.

Walter Bush may be one of the few people in all of hockey who never had an enemy. I don't know of anyone who doesn't like him. I honestly cannot think of anyone in management who is as widely liked and respected. I first got to know him when I played for the University of Minnesota. He played hockey for Dartmouth and hasn't left the game since. He was widely known as a hockey administrator who, through his devotion and hard work, was recognized as playing an integral part in the development of the national and international amateur game.

Walter was one of the founders of the Minnesota Amateur Hockey Association. In 1959 he became the team manager for the U.S. National Hockey Team as well as director of the U.S. Olympic Hockey Committee. By 1964 he was the general manager of the U.S. Olympic Team. He later became the owner and president of the Minneapolis Bruins of the Central Hockey League, a farm club of the Boston Bruins.

With Walter's leadership skills and respected reputation in hockey, it didn't take long for the Twin Cities to gain a National Hockey League expansion team. Walter was the president of the Minnesota North Stars from 1966 to 1976 and chairman of the board from 1976 to 1978.

In 1965 Walter was heavily involved in USA Hockey and came to talk to me about a hockey trip. He was putting together a team to play a few exhibition games in the Soviet Union and he wanted me to be on the team. That was my first brush with both Walter and USA Hockey. He asked me later to join the U.S. Olympic Team for the 1968 Games, asking if I wanted American citizenship. Walter, along with Murray Williamson, was the driving force behind my citizenship, getting a bill through Congress to make it happen quickly. I will always be indebted.

After the Games were over, I was negotiating to play professional hockey with the North Stars and we just couldn't get the
contract done. Walter was the team president and he finally called
me into his office. We ultimately worked out a personal services
contract in which I would be involved in public appearances as well
as setting up the North Stars' hockey school and running it. The
third part of it allowed them to sell my services to Colwell Press.
Colwell had the advertising and program rights and I would be part
of their sales team.

We finally reached an agreement when I wrote down *$120,000
total* on a piece of paper for a three-year contract. Walter wrote
$110,000. We settled on *$116,000,* and I became a Minnesota
North Star.

When I signed that contract, I figured I would retire from hockey
and go back to work at the end of it. Little did I know I would still
be with the North Stars 23 years later. I had heard on two occasions
that Wren Blair and then Jack Gordon tried to trade me and both
times the owners of the team said no. I am certain Walter had a lot to
do with that, as well as Gordy Ritz and Bob McNulty.

Walter got me involved with USA Hockey in 1978 and I am still
on its international council and foundation board today.

Walter is a warm, caring human being. He is very affable, a great
storyteller, and extremely kind and generous. He is considerate and
thoughtful—a truly unique individual.

• • •

I really believe that most people have a significant person who
impacted their lives. I know I certainly have been fortunate to have
had many in mine. Another is Glen Sonmor.

Glen played in the National Hockey League for two years with
the New York Rangers. He played left wing and was known throughout the league as a very physical player who had a reputation for his

fighting abilities. His playing career was ended abruptly when he suffered a serious eye injury after being hit with a teammate's slap shot. But he stayed in the game he loved.

When you know Glen Sonmor, you learn very quickly that you want him with you if you decide to go to war. He will support you, fight for you, and is as deeply loyal a person as you will ever find. I first met Glen when he was hired as the head hockey coach for the University of Minnesota. I had finished my eligibility as a player and was coaching the Minnesota freshman team under John Mariucci. Anytime I get the chance to talk about Glen Sonmor, I have to start out by saying that he is a wonderful human being. He is also another on the long list of hockey fanatics.

When Glen took over as coach of the Gophers, we hit it off right away, and we have remained friends for almost 50 years. Glen is a tough, competitive guy; a tremendous leader; and has a devoted interest in education. He is intelligent, has incredible stamina, and, in my opinion, is the best coach the Minnesota North Stars ever had.

He is one of those guys whose remarkable love for the game is coupled with a never-ending burning desire to win. He is a great motivator and a coach who really understands the game from every angle. He knew how to beat opponents.

Glen always had the ability to make players play tougher and want to go to battle for him. He was a solid, committed coach who never gave less than all he had every single day of his career. He had the knowledge to help players to perform better than they actually were. And he always stressed the fundamentals of the game.

Glen would practice his teams hard and stress the fundamentals ("No player goes offside!"). He taught his men how to play the game and learn the important yet often forgotten aspects of the game. He wanted them to be physical ("Get on the outside of the check, not the inside.").

Glen was very loyal to his players and would back them to a fault. I remember an opposing coach once yelling at one of our players. Glen fired right back to him, "You keep that up and I'll come over there and beat the —— out of you!"

His team truly believed in him. They stood behind him no matter what. This fact was evident during one of the biggest brawls to ever take place in NHL history.

We had been dominated by the Boston Bruins for years. Before a game with the Bruins, the Boston newspapers had called us "soft" because of the way we played against their local favorites. I remember Glen calling me before the game and telling me that the team had "to take a stand" at this game if we were going to ever have a chance of beating Boston.

"Louie has been a godsend in my life. He was always there for me. He never let me down. I can honestly say, without him standing beside me I don't know what would have happened to me. He has always been a wonderful friend."

—GLEN SONMOR, FORMER HEAD COACH, MINNESOTA NORTH STARS AND UNIVERSITY OF MINNESOTA GOPHERS

I agreed and Glen had a meeting with the team before the game. He told them that we were all through allowing Boston to push us around. He wrote down the Bruins roster and showed the team how our roster matched up with theirs where it came to toughness. He went on to tell them that the first sign of intimidation would be the signal that we were going to battle.

As it turns out, it only took six seconds—then one of the most infamous brawls in hockey history ignited. Glen knew what he had to do and the team responded. We lost the game that night but used it as impetus to win two playoff games in Boston a few weeks later. Come to think of it, I think that game in Boston that night may have been the only time in my career as a coach and general manager that I was happy after a loss.

As a final note on that night in Boston, when the fight was finally over, Glen was hollering at Boston coach Gerry Cheevers, "Cheevers, if I get my hands on you, your head is going home in a basket. We can finish this right here, just you and me!" That was Glen; he was right in there with the players every step of the way, and they loved him for it.

You could go searching for a long time and it would be hard to find anyone as enthusiastic as Glen Sonmor. He is 80 years old, and pure and simple, he loves the game. No one loves Gopher hockey more than Glen Sonmor, and you can tell that by listening to a few minutes of his color commentary on the Minnesota games. He has also scouted for the Minnesota Wild. He just has to be involved in hockey in some way, and he always does a great job in whatever role he takes. After he left the Wild, I called my good friend Glen Sather of the Rangers and he hired Sonmor, who said to me, "Louie, isn't it wonderful that I am going to go through my whole life without ever working?"

Glen is a tremendous hockey scout and an incredible judge of talent. When it comes to hockey, he is a workaholic no matter what the job. He has an unbelievable passion for the game that burns inside him. Without a doubt, hockey has been his greatest enjoyment in life. As long as he is around it, he is happy.

As time goes by the years start to run together, and the time you spend with someone you care about rushes by you. With Glen Sonmor, we have been friends for 50 years and have been through a lot together. I treasure every second of it. I am a fortunate person to have been associated with Glen Sonmor for so long a time.

Herb Brooks was another of my favorite people. As a player Brooks played for the Minnesota Gophers from 1955 to 1959 and was on the U.S. Olympic Hockey Team in 1964 and again with me in 1968. And, of course, he was also the coach of the 1980 team.

I asked Herbie to take over my freshman coaching job. After the Olympics, I told him that if I signed with the North Stars, he should take my job as the freshman coach at the University of Minnesota. So I talked to Glen Sonmor, who was the varsity coach at the time, and Marsh Ryman, who was the athletic director. Glen supported it, so Herbie had to go and sit down with Ryman about the job.

I told him, "Now look, Herbie, you can get $1,000 to coach the freshmen. That's what they're paying me, so don't you back off of that price or I will choke you! Marsh will try to sign you for less money, but don't give in to him." Herbie agreed and went in to meet with Ryman. After the meeting, I asked him, "How did it go?"

He said, "It went great. Everything is fine."

> "When it comes to competitiveness, Lou goes to the top of the list. And Lou is without a doubt the best family man I have ever known. There is nothing more important to him than his family."
>
> —GLEN SATHER, GENERAL MANAGER, NEW YORK RANGERS

I could tell from the way he said it that he was leaving something out. "Okay, what is it?" I said to him. "You are lying to me, now what happened?"

He looked at me sheepishly and said, "I got $800."

Herbie was a great coach. He went on to coach the varsity teams at Minnesota to three national championships.

During our Olympic year, the director of player personnel for the Detroit Red Wings asked if I would be interested in signing a contract with them. Because expansion was coming, every NHL team had to reduce their reserve list and I was now a free agent. Herbie was with me at the time and piped into the conversation, "Listen, any contracts that are signed here include me. Lou and I go together as a package deal. If you take Lou, you have to take me too."

The director looked at Herbie and said, "Okay, we'll sign you and you can be trade bait for us in the American Hockey League."

Herbie and I enjoyed our times together. We were co-captains of the Olympic Team and roommates. We played together in Rochester and used to ride to the games together twice a week. We received $5 for gas; he was paid $25 per game and I got $30. Of course, times have changed since then!

When I first became the general manager of the North Stars in February 1978, I wanted Herbie to be the coach. We got to the contract negotiating stage and we had a difference between us in the length of the contract. Herb wanted three years and I wanted to give him two. "I have two, you're getting two," I told him.

He said to me, "Louie, listen now, go talk to the boss. You can get me three years." I said back to him, "Herb, don't be so stubborn, I *am* the boss and you're getting two!"

We couldn't get the deal done so Herbie said, "Louie, what I really want is to be the coach of the Olympic Team. Can you help me get that job?" I did what I could. And, well, it happened for Herbie— and history was made.

Over the years, I have tried to assist him in getting various jobs in hockey but there always seems to be some stumbling block keeping Herbie from taking them. Once I negotiated for him to take a job with the Rangers for a contract of over $1 million per year. He turned it down. Then later he came to me asking for help getting a job coaching the USA Junior Team in the world championships. He wanted $25,000 to coach and they wanted to give him $15,000; he wanted my help getting the extra $10,000.

I told him, "Herbie, you turned down the more than $1 million that I had for you to coach the Rangers and now you want me to help you get $25,000? What's the matter with you?"

Another time I told him I was upset that he would consider taking $300,000 to coach in the Soviet Union while he left the millions on the table in the NHL. But that was Herbie. He always made things interesting.

I had many of these negotiations in the financial business too. I think Herbie would have really excelled in that. In fact, I offered him a job working with me once. He said he wanted to, but then said, "next year." He just had trouble at times deciding what he should do. But I will tell you this—once he decided what he wanted, he drove himself to succeed at it and there was never a doubt about his commitment.

Just before he died, we had talked about the possibility of him going to New York again to coach the Rangers. Although my friend Glen Sather had been turned down by Herbie before, Glen was considering adding him to his staff.

Herbie came to my office and asked me to ride with him to the Hall of Fame golf tournament, but I was traveling to New Jersey at the time and couldn't make it with him. So he went by himself and died in a car accident on his way back. By the time I got off the plane in Philadelphia, I recall having 25 to 30 messages on my cell phone. I can't help thinking that he might still be alive today if I had made the trip with him.

During all the years in the National Hockey League, I have known some great coaches and administrators. Many of these gifted individuals became my associates and friends.

In my opinion, the best hockey coach that I ever knew was Scotty Bowman. Scotty Bowman won nine Stanley Cups in his years as coach of the Montreal Canadiens, Pittsburgh Penguins, and the Detroit Red Wings. He holds the record for most wins as a coach during the NHL regular season with 1,244 and also with wins in playoff games (223). Those totals are absolutely amazing. And actually you could make it 11 Cups if you count the two years that he served as director of player development and as a consultant with Pittsburgh and Detroit. I have chased one my whole career.

Scotty Bowman had a tremendous feel for the pulse of the game. He knew how to get the most out of his players and was an incredible game tactician. He had a great understanding of his opponents and of his own personnel. He was so knowledgeable about the game and knew which buttons to push to motivate his teams. He must have been doing all of it the right way; the results speak for themselves.

Another of the coaching greats is Al Arbour. Al was a player in the NHL for 14 years and then a coach for St. Louis and then the New York Islanders. He won four consecutive Stanley Cup championships from 1980 to 1983—a phenomenal accomplishment.

Al was a terrific coach and motivator. A player for more than two decades, he thoroughly understood every aspect of the game and did a superb job of teaching his players to play well as a unit. Arbour was popular with his players and his philosophy of coaching was very successful. And obviously, it worked for his Islanders.

My third choice in the coaching ranks would be Herb Brooks. He was extremely successful at preparing his team to play and there was never any question about their conditioning. Even in practices he was not afraid to drive them. He refused to let an opponent outwork his players. Herbie loved to have a team skilled in skating and puck control.

Of course, there are others who have been great in their profession. I must give credit to some of the great general managers that I know who have had an impact on the game and my life. Each of them has been superb in their responsibilities, their expertise, and their exemplary professionalism. I am speaking of Glen Sather, Cliff Fletcher, Harry Sinden, Bill Torrey, Bob Pulford, Bobby Clarke, Pat Quinn, Dave Poile, and Emile Francis. These men have long been thought of as iconic figures in professional hockey. They understand the game, love it, and have had a wonderful impact on it for most of their lives. It has truly been my distinct honor and privilege to know each of them.

• • •

When I think back to my days in the Soo, one of the first people that comes to mind is Angelo Bumbacco, our mentor and manager. He was like a father to all the kids in town and our success was an important part of his life. I try to see him whenever I visit. He is still involved in hockey and serves as an amateur scout for the Tampa Bay Lightning. As youngsters, we all hung around Bumbacco's store and listened to the older guys discuss sports, especially hockey.

"Lou Nanne is an extremely confident person and one of the most competitive individuals I have ever met. He is always fun to be around. He has a great outgoing personality and is always making you laugh about something."

—Bob Pulford, former general manager, Chicago Blackhawks

When I was a kid, I was very small. I used to get into everything. I was overly hyper and could not sit still. A couple of times some of the older fellows locked me in the pop cooler. Once they taped me to a supporting post in the store to slow me down. Others used to give me "zellies"— taking their big knuckles and snapping them off my head. That really bugged me. I used to go over to my friend Pat Nardini's house to lift weights. I would motivate myself by picturing the day the zellies would stop. I was going to put an end to it. Sure enough, I can remember the time that they weren't able to do it to me anymore. I was 16 and I was strong enough to stop it, even though they were doing it for pure fun.

Angelo would never mistreat anybody. He is a tremendously caring person and he was the first coach I ever had in organized hockey. When I was growing up, every player that ever came out of

Sault Ste. Marie played for him. He was an incredible influence on my life and I will never forget what he did for me. I have the highest regard for him as a coach and manager and as a special person in my life.

He was the one many years back who got the affiliation with the Chicago Blackhawks whereby they obtained the rights to those who were playing for the Blackhawks, Contractors, and Greyhounds. He cared so much about all of us. If you go to his home, you will see pictures of all the guys in the Soo who made it to the NHL. We were his life and he was so proud of all of us who did well in hockey. He was the one that made sure each one of us got the chance to play the sport he loved. Gene Ubriaco, Chico and Wayne Maki, Matt Ravlich, Phil and Tony Esposito, Ron Francis, Jerry Korab, Jim Wiley, Ivan Boldirev, and I are all Soo boys who played for Ang.

My list of great athletes and associates and friends could go on forever and take up a few more books. These are just a few. To the many others who have influenced my life, a heartfelt thank you.

7

Lowest of Lows, Highest of Highs

There has never been another night like it. The electrifying intensity in the building will stay with me for the rest of my life. It has been almost 30 years since we met the New York Islanders in the third game of the Stanley Cup finals, and yet in my heart and soul, it seems like it was only yesterday. A current of tremendous emotion and passion ran through the players, coaches, and fans. It was beyond anything I had ever witnessed in hockey. I have played and watched big games in arenas all over the world. Nothing came close; it was absolutely riveting!

Given my intense competitive nature—and being involved in hockey for as long as I have—I've experienced some extremely high highs and extraordinarily low lows. One of the biggest disappointments was losing in the Stanley Cup Finals to the New York Islanders in 1981. There is no question that the Islanders should have captured the Cup; they were a better team than we were. But to get that close and not win it was devastating.

The Islanders were a fantastic team with extraordinary talent. Mike Bossy, the great right winger, scored 50 goals in his first 50 games for New York that year. Denis Potvin was one of the finest defensive players of all time, and Bryan Trottier was one of the most incredible players to ever play professional hockey. Clark Gillies was a top-notch power forward in. In the goal was Billy Smith, who was dominant during the regular season and in the playoffs. Al Arbour, their outstanding coach, had them operating on all cylinders and they had peaked during their playoff run. They were the whole package.

The Islanders had players with tremendous skills and they were also a very physical and tough team. They had great penalty killing with Butch Goring. During the first playoff game they were able to score two short-handed goals against us.

Put simply, they were a complete team. They had some of the best players in the league and they were excellently coached. It was a very difficult challenge but we were there in the finals with them, and the Stanley Cup was right in front of our very eyes.

When you start a season, winning the Stanley Cup at the end is the ultimate goal for every team. When you make it to the finals, you look around and see that every team in the National Hockey League has failed to accomplish their goal except for you and your opponent. It's such a long season and such a difficult climb; to be one of the last two standing is a tremendous accomplishment. As a player or general manager, you know how difficult it was just to get there. So once you do get there, the realization hits you that you must take advantage of the opportunity because you may never get there again.

After we lost to the Islanders in five games, all I could think at the time was that we might never get again. That was the hardest thing to take. The fact of the matter was, it would be another decade before we returned to the Stanley Cup finals.

I was so proud of our team because they worked hard all season long and played so well in the playoffs. It was a difficult loss to take, but not nearly as difficult as it would have been if we had been the better team and lost.

Glen Sonmor did a magnificent job of coaching and really had the team ready to play. We just didn't have enough in our tank to compete with them. It was a big opportunity for us to win it and we didn't do it. And to this day, it bothers me that I was never a part of a Stanley Cup championship.

We had an outstanding team that year. Bobby Smith, Steve Payne, Al MacAdam, Dino Ciccarelli, Craig Hartsburg, Neal Broten, Gil Meloche, Don Beaupre, and many others were excellent players. We had good team leadership and great camaraderie.

I really thought we were going to be a team of destiny that year because we had gone through so much throughout the season and playoffs in order to get to the finals. I honestly thought we had a chance to win it all—and then the bubble burst. I was happy for the guys that they played so well, but so sad that they were not able to win the Stanley Cup championship.

After it was over, I racked my brain about what we could have done differently that might have made the difference in winning and losing. *If only this could have happened. If only that could have happened.* On and on, over and over in my mind, I rehashed everything, but the outcome was always the same. The game has to be played on the ice. It never works to replay it in your mind and wish for a different conclusion. In the end, we lost. And it still hurts.

The only thing that brings consolation to me when I think back on that great run is that I know in my heart the Islanders were just better than us. It was as true then as it is now.

One of my most vivid recollections of that series was the third game, which was played at the Met Center. We had lost the first two on the Island and were determined to even the series at home. What happened that night is something I will never forget. The noise, intensity, emotion, and fervor of all the fans—it made for a remarkable event. It was unlike anything I had ever witnessed before or after.

I can see the game in my head like it's a film playing frame by frame. I am right there. And the noise is deafening. I honestly don't believe there has ever been a louder building in all of professional hockey than the Met Center was that night. In the locker room, you could hear the noise and feel the rumbling from inside the arena. It got louder and louder in the hour leading up to the game. I guarantee you that there isn't a person who was at that game who doesn't remember what it felt like to be at the Met Center that night.

I can still see the tremendous crowd, all of them on their feet and screaming at the top of their lungs. I can feel the electricity like it is shooting through my veins—and that was almost 30 years ago! It was unforgettable. I've always said that the Met Center had the most rabid fans in all of sports. Minnesota fans love hockey; that is a given. And they were there that night in full force. It felt like a heavyweight championship fight.

It had been a beautiful day outside in the spring of the year, and many fans seized the opportunity to tailgate in the parking lot for several hours leading up to the game. The fun and excitement started early that day. Everyone was in a good mood. Everyone was excited. *We were going to win this thing!*

But we didn't. We lost the game, despite an incredible effort by the North Stars. We should have won the game. We had plenty of chances. But we lost. Looking back at that game, I felt like it was the only game in the playoff series that we should have won. But we gave it our best, that's for sure.

I had every one of my obsessions and superstitions in full force that night. I walked around my chair this way and that. I watched from the press box, sat in my chair a certain way. I went upstairs. I went downstairs. I went places where I couldn't see the game. Then I would go back upstairs again, back down and then back up. I would hold the chair a certain way—anything to win the game, but nothing worked.

After the game, I couldn't leave. I stayed at the Met Center and had a drink with Glen and Murray Oliver and talked it all over. The next thing I knew, it was 2:00 in the morning. And then I went home, talked some more, and was up until 4:00.

It was an unbelievable night, one that will always stay with me. I only wish the game and the series had ended in our favor. It would have been on the high side of my ledger instead of the low side.

The only other experience that I have ever had that would even come close to that night was a decade later at the 1991 All-Star Game in Chicago. The United States had just entered into the Gulf War at the time and the country was really pulling together. It was a patriotic night, and you could feel it in the air—the crowd was unified. The game was at Chicago Stadium. The lights were turned out, the organ was blaring, and suddenly everyone was overcome. As the national anthem began, a feeling ran through everyone there. In all my years in professional sports, these were the two most memorable nights of my life.

There was another time in hockey history that ranks up there with those two games, and that was the upset of the Soviet team at Lake Placid by the U.S. Olympic Team in 1980. But the situation was so different. In that game, no one had expected the Americans to prevail. In fact, in a game two weeks before, the Soviets had destroyed the United States 10–3. The intensity of the Olympic crowd didn't hold a candle to the fans that night at the Met Center, or even in Chicago. Now the crowd got to a fever pitch as the game went on, but it took a while for that to happen.

Another factor, of course, is the game attendance. Lake Placid Arena was only a third of the size of the Met Center. The championship game was a huge one for the American team, no doubt about that, but there was such a small expectation of victory. Toward the end of the game, with the U.S. in the lead, the noise became deafening. And in the end, it was pure bedlam.

• • •

The toughest loss I faced in my career was against the Chicago Blackhawks. They knocked us out of the 1982 playoffs—the year after our Stanley Cup appearance. After losing to the Islanders in the previous season, we came back and had a tremendous regular season. We won the division title and were set to make another run at the Cup. Our first opponent in the playoffs was the Chicago Blackhawks, a team that had finished more than 20 points below us in the standings. We were the heavy favorites to win the series and advance in the playoffs. Everyone said we would win it.

We had a very strong team and we played so well in the series. That made it hurt even more. As I have said many times, losses are always tough, but when you lose even after you play well, they are the toughest to take. You keep asking yourself, *What went wrong? What could we have done differently to change the outcome?* Well, when you play badly, the answer is simple: *We played badly. We stunk up the place.*

But in the Chicago series, we hadn't played badly. We should have won. We played great and we lost. And the reason we lost was Murray Bannerman. Chicago had Bannerman in the nets and he was literally stealing games from us. We were playing well enough to win but Bannerman just simply closed the door on us. He stopped everything, I mean everything. It was almost unfair, the way he played.

Our guys played hard in every game. Many of the so-called experts had picked the North Stars to defeat Chicago, move through the playoffs, and win the Stanley Cup that year. The series against Chicago was supposed to be just a tune-up for the championship run.

We were playing so well and even though the series was close because of Bannerman, I always believed we were still going to win. After all we were playing a team that had finished far below us in the regular-season standings. When we lost to the Blackhawks, I absolutely could not believe it. It was the worst sinking feeling I had ever experienced at a hockey game in my life. I was devastated. But that was it. We lost and were out of the playoffs.

After the game, I went down to the team dressing room and said a few things to the players. I said, "I want you to go home and think about this. I want you to think about what happened here tonight. I want you to each remember this sick feeling and how lousy it is. I want you to make sure that this never happens again."

Then, a few weeks later, Glen and I were at a board of directors meeting with the owners, and one of the owner advisors who was in attendance asked us, "What happened? We want to be sure that this never happens again."

Glen and I kind of looked at him in amazement, like we didn't understand what he was saying. I mean, did he think he was telling us something we didn't already think about? It wasn't the Gunds, the team owners telling us this. As usual, they were great. It was one of their advisors, some guy who thought he had all the answers. He said to us again, "We don't want this to happen again." I thought Glen was going to jump across the table and go after him. Getting beaten by Chicago was bad enough. We didn't need admonishment from some team advisor!

I really didn't plan any major changes for the team after that loss, as it happened. After all, we had a great season, and we had some outstanding players who played together very well. What kept going through my mind every day wasn't the future, anyway—it was the goals we missed in the series. We had so many chances and simply could not get past Bannerman. He kept making save after save, keeping us out of the nets. I had to put it to rest and begin planning for the next season, but I couldn't get my mind off it.

There I was, one season away from losing to the Islanders, and the same things were going through my mind. *How did we miss all of those opportunities?* The loss to Chicago hit me so much harder than the Islanders loss, because we were a much better team than the Blackhawks.

The season was so long and taxing. There were so many games, so much travel, and for what? We had to start the whole thing all over again. All of the work, all of the effort, all of the preparation, and all for naught. I knew what it would take to get there again. It just seemed so overwhelming to have to start at the beginning. It was just too much.

Recently I was talking about the series with Chicago and how much the playoff loss had devastated me, and I was asked how long it took for me to finally get over it. Believe me when I say, the question raised such acute ire in me. It took me right back there to three decades ago and I shouted out, "I'M NOT OVER IT!" I honestly don't think I ever will be. The moment that question was asked, that sick feeling came over me again.

Sometimes I look at other professional teams, knowing what they must be going through when things go badly for them. Growing up in the Soo, my favorite hockey team was the Detroit Red Wings and my favorite football team was always the Detroit Lions. I think about how difficult it must have been for the Lions organization—the players, coaches, and staff—when they went 0–16 in 2008. They lost every single regular-season game! I wonder how they handled it. They went through the off-season, with all the hours of planning and preparation. They went through training camp and the preseason, with all of the roster changes and decisions and the countless hours of work. And then they started the regular season and played the games, scouted their opponents, and spent endless hours on the practice field in preparation for each and every one of the 16 games on their

During training camp for the 1968 U.S. Olympic Team.

North Stars general manager Wren Blair and I discuss my contract at a Brainerd, MN, resort in 1967.

My first individual photo taken with the North Stars, Detroit 1968.

My very first North Stars team.

Réjean Houle of the Montreal Canadiens checking me, as Murray Oliver looks on.

Getting a shot on net against the St. Louis Blues, Gary Unger trails the play.

My wife, Francine, cheers me on at a North Stars game.

Checking the great Bobby Hull of the Chicago Blackhawks in 1968.

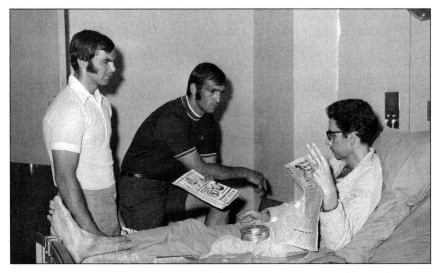

Barry Gibbs and I visiting a patient during our 1972 USO hospital tour in Japan.

(Above) Vacationing in Las Vegas after the 1971 season with J.P. Parise, Tom Reid, Gump Worsley and Bill Goldsworthy, and our wives.

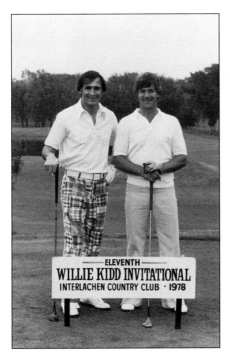

(Above) I had the privilege of presenting Gump Worsley at his Hockey Hall of Fame induction in Toronto.

(Left) With my partner Bobby Orr playing in the Willie Kidd Invitational at Interlachen Country Club.

Bill Torrey (left), Cliff Fletcher (second from right) and me at Harry Sinden's (second from left) induction into the Hockey Hall of Fame.

Enjoying a North Stars alumni game at the Met Center.

Our Minnesota Golden Gophers Alumni Team in 1993.

My hero, Gordie Howe, and I before a Heroes of Hockey game at Madison Square Garden.

Our family photo taken with my mother-in-law (center) at her 90th birthday party.

schedule. And then they lost every one. It had to be absolute devastation. I feel for them and what they went through. We never experienced anything quite like that, but I do know well that feeling that comes with the losses.

In hockey, we had the ability to trade players. I made countless numbers of trades in my career as general manager of the North Stars, but in football there are not a lot of trades made throughout the season. We always had a chance to shuffle the deck if we needed to. It has to be a different mind-set in football, when you know you have the same faces in that locker room all season long.

When I was the general manager, I always wanted to win and win *right now*. In my mind there is never any time for losing, so I did whatever to improve the team. And I was always willing to tinker if we felt the team could be improved.

I recall years earlier, when I was player, and we lost a playoff series to the St. Louis Blues in the final playoff game. It was overtime. I can still see the puck go in the net—and I still have the same sick feeling whenever I think about it. I can describe what happened like I was the play-by-play voice for the game. I can see their wing, Kevin O'Shea, firing a shot at our goalie Cesare Maniago from the top of the circle on the far wing. I can see the puck hit the pipe, hit Cesare in the back, and trickle into the net. And just like that it was over.

I didn't know what to do. The crowd went silent and there was a hush over the entire arena. I was not at all prepared for a loss. The same is true with the Chicago series. I planned and prepared and was ready and excited to win but was never prepared to lose.

After the game, several of us were going out to eat. We went over to the Decathlon Club, but none of us had an appetite. We didn't know what to do with ourselves. We were not prepared for tomorrow because *tomorrow we were supposed to be playing hockey*. You can gather up the pieces and try to move on, but the hurt stays with you.

Losing, whether you are a player or general manager, felt the same to me. It didn't matter what my role was—I just hate losing, pure and simple. Very early on in my hockey career, as a youngster, I got accustomed to winning—because we never lost. We had great players on all of our teams and we always won. I got used to it and I liked it. We won in softball. We won in baseball. We won in hockey. Winning was regular for us. Except for the grade school game, when I was eleven years old and Jimmy Sanko beat us with a goal in overtime, of course. I still get upset thinking about it. Maybe there will come a time when I will get over it and forgive Jimmy. But it hasn't happened yet—and it's been 58 years!

Ultimately, I got my fair share of devastation in hockey, facing some difficult defeats in big games. There is no question about that. But I need to say this about those losses and all that comes with them: there has been great balance in my life. I have been extremely fortunate to have been blessed with the physical abilities that I have, to have been able to play the sport that I love for so many years, and then to stay on in management.

Growing up in Sault Ste. Marie, and being involved in the winning tradition of the Soo teams and knowing all of the great people and coaches that I had, was a wonderful experience. I got to do the things that I truly loved to do.

Then I had the incredible opportunity to attend college at the University of Minnesota and play hockey for the Gophers. There I met John Mariucci, who became one of the great influences of my life. Many of the highest points in my career came during my time playing with Minnesota. I was a 1963 first-team All-Star. I was the WCHA Most Valuable Player in 1963, an NCAA West first-team All-American in 1963, and was the first defenseman in the history of the WCHA to win the overall scoring championship. In addition, I was captain of the Gophers hockey team and also voted to the

WCHA's Top 50 Players in 50 Years team. All of them are milestones in my playing career that I will cherish forever.

My years at the university were followed by the opportunity to play some minor league hockey for a few years before becoming a member of Olympic Team. I cannot even begin to express the feeling that I had to represent the United States in the Olympic Games; there is just not a high that supersedes it.

After that, I had the opportunity to sign a contract with the Minnesota North Stars to play professionally in the National Hockey League. I can never put much focus on the lows of my career when I take the time to reflect on the highs I have had. I was a professional hockey player. It can't get much better than that.

As a young boy, my dream was to play for the Sault Ste. Marie Greyhounds. That was it. Well, I didn't play on our senior team but I did have the opportunity to do so much more—with the Gophers, the U.S. Olympic Team and the North Stars.

There were so many highs. Even though we lost that huge series in the Stanley Cup Finals in 1981 to the New York Islanders—and that was a tremendous low—it was a high for me because we were there. To play in the Stanley Cup finals is a goal few achieve in life.

In fact, we almost pulled off a miracle. In 1971 we upset St. Louis in the first round of the playoffs and then faced the great Montreal Canadiens team in cross-division play. No team from the original 1967 expansion had beaten one of the Original Six teams in the playoffs. Each year the established NHL teams would sweep their series en route the Stanley Cup. This was the first year of crossover play, so we had to win the series over Montreal to go to the finals—and we almost did.

The experts predicted we would lose in four games. But we changed things. We beat the Canadiens in Montreal and I got the winning goal in the game. It was an unbelievable feeling. The Canadiens were up 3–2 with the sixth game set for the Met Center.

With Montreal leading in Game 6 3–2, we thought Ted Hampson had scored for us in the last second to tie and force the game into overtime. However, the ruling was that the puck crossed the goal line after the buzzer. The series ended and Montreal went onto the finals. Still, it was unreal for us to have gone that far and to have become the first newly franchised team to win a playoff game against an established team. And beating the Canadiens in Montreal to accomplish it was magnificent, and a memory for the vault that holds the highest of highs.

I enjoyed my years as a player in the National Hockey League so much. Then, to have what followed in a decade in the general manager's role was almost hard to fathom. I know that my drive to win was very hard on me overall, but the opportunities afforded to me and the many friendships made in the process certainly made it a fabulous experience.

For one thing, my hockey exploits presented me with a lifestyle that afforded me the pleasures of traveling all over the world doing something that I loved. I had come a long way from playing street hockey in front of the house in Sault Ste. Marie. It had been a long time since I had heard mom yelling, "Louie, you're late again!" Yet I can still hear her words. "Yeah, Mom, but I got 12 goals!" And her reply, "Well, okay then." And it has been a long time since I heard my dad say, "That's it, Louie, if you get cut one more time and I have to take you in for stitches, don't come home!"

I've certainly given much of my life to hockey over the years. But for what I've given, hockey has given me as much in return.

8

Behind the Microphone

I climbed aboard and started the interview. I didn't think much about it at the time, but if the amount of people who have mentioned it to me over the years is any indication, it may have been the most famous interview of all time!

I believe I may be the first and perhaps the only broadcaster in all of sports who talked to a Zamboni driver while riding the machine. We did it between periods of the Minnesota State Boys High School Hockey Tournament back in the mid-'60s. I just thought people might like to know about the machine and what the driver had to do in resurfacing the ice between periods of a hockey game. I had no idea it would get the attention that it did.

One of my many duties is providing color commentary for the State Boys High School Hockey Tournament, which I have been doing since 1964. It is hard for me to fathom that last March was my 46th year! It has been a remarkable run and one that I have enjoyed immensely. What has made it even more special was that in this past year my grandson played in the tournament. My son had played before him in the tournament, too. So I have now broadcasted games for the both of them. There have not been many thrills in my life greater than that. And fortunately, both of their teams won the state championship.

I honestly don't remember how my broadcasting career started. I don't know if someone recommended me, or if WTCN even knew that I might be interested. I had completed my hockey eligibility at the University of Minnesota in June 1963 and was in a contract dispute with the Chicago Blackhawks, who had owned my rights in the National Hockey League because of their affiliation with the teams in Sault Ste. Marie.

I was playing hockey on the weekends in Rochester and coaching the university freshman team. One day, right out of the blue, I got a call to come over to the WTCN studios. There was a little discussion about doing some broadcasting and a brief audition, and I was asked if I would be interested in doing the color commentary for the Boys High School Hockey Tournament. I thought it sounded fun, so I agreed to do the game analysis and provide the commentary. I never thought that I would still be doing it decades later. And best of all, I had absolutely no idea how much enjoyment I would get from it! It has been wonderful in every respect. I have loved doing the games and have had such tremendous passion for the tournament.

Of course, when I started I had no idea what being a hockey color commentator might entail. I had no experience, so I worked off of the expert advice I received from longtime television icon Mel Jass. After I agreed to the post, I was taken downstairs to the studio, which is where I first met Mel. Most residents of the Twin Cities in the 1960s certainly remember Mel, his "Midday Matinee" movies, and his famous line—"Oh, you have a good job!"

Mel was a genius of the airwaves but he used to take a lot of kidding about his famous line. "And what do you do for a living?" he would ask. The person he was interviewing might say, "Well, Mel, I work on a farm, and the majority of the day my job is to go around and pick up horse manure." Mel would respond by saying, "Oh, you have a good job!" It always went something like that. But he meant it.

Mel gave some really great advice to a kid who was green in broadcasting. He told me, "Lou, when you are talking into the camera, look at the red light and just think of someone standing in their living room and you with him, just having a discussion." I have never forgotten that and it has been a great help to me in all my years of broadcasting.

I remember doing a commercial with Bill Goldsworthy and every time the red light on the camera would go on to start the commercial, Goldy would not be able to talk. He would just stutter and stammer. The light really did him in. Finally after about the eighth take, I told him about the advice Mel Jass had given me and it worked. We finally were able to do the commercial.

In the beginning, it was difficult. I had never done anything even remotely like it before. But it was terrific. I worked with Frank Buetel and we did absolutely everything. There was basically just the two of us. Frank and I did the games, the interviews between periods, and the postgame interviews. Through the years, I have worked with numerous play-by-play broadcasters and always had a good time with whomever I worked with. Last year after the 2009 tournament, we received an Emmy Award, and it was quite an honor for us all.

I had a crew cut when I did my first broadcast and I still get grief over that. I think people have forgotten that when I started doing the state tournament games I was just a kid myself. I think I was probably entitled to wear a crew cut.

I have developed a philosophy that I try to stay with when I broadcast the games. I am not big into statistics and have told the people I work with, "If you want statistics out there, put them on the screen." I feel I don't have time to rattle off a bunch of numbers for the listeners because of all the commercials; my job is to apprise them of what is happening during the game. In addition I want to let them know what has just happened, what should happen, or what will be happening as the game goes on.

It is very rewarding to have people enjoy my broadcasting work. People will come up to me and tell me stories that connect them to one of my telecasts. That really means a great deal to me because it is one of my great passions. To know that people like what I do is very special.

Oftentimes people have told me, "Lou, don't ever quit the state tournament. You do a great job!" or "I grew up with you watching the state hockey tourney," or "You have made me a better fan of hockey by watching and listening to you at tournament time." When I hear feedback like that, it really makes it all worthwhile.

When I am broadcasting, I like to stay away from the negatives. To me, it's okay to highlight and bring up mistakes but I never focus on an individual making them. Hockey is a game of mistakes. If you cause players to become afraid of making them, they will only make more. So I just don't do it in my analysis of the youngsters' play. I will point out how a player and team capitalize on those mistakes; it is important to show how the plays originated.

The highlight of the state high school hockey tournament continues to be the tremendous passion that these kids bring to it. They work so hard and represent their schools wonderfully. The fans have as much passion as the players do, and want their school to be winners. They are loyal as can be. It's a one-of-a-kind experience. It is great to have been a part of all of this for so long and to watch the skill level improve year after year.

The excitement and intensity in the building is electric. I just marvel at it. It is so incredible to see the energy and emotion and always sad to see teams lose. I wish every team could win because the kids play so hard and never give up. They are all deserving! But win or lose, their experiences will remain with them forever.

As the tournament time gets closer, I try to see as many of the teams as possible. I talk to the coaches and start my preparation. I want to know the teams that are likely going to make the tournament and I begin to focus on some of the key players. I can never get to see all the teams that make it in, but I try to get familiar with as many as I can so that I have an idea of their strengths and weaknesses.

Once the tournament starts, I spend time watching team warm-ups. I figure out how they have their lines set up and get to know each player by number and shooting side. I make a point of talking to the coaches and to ask them their thoughts about their opponents. I take a lot of notes and do quite a bit of memory work so that I am fully prepared to bring the best possible game analysis to the viewers and listeners once the games begin. I want to know the teams' tendencies and what players we should be paying special attention to during the game. It's all part of a process that I go through to be ready for the beginning of the games. I treasure every minute of it.

The games are now set up with two brackets, Single A and Double A. The system is much better than it is in basketball, with all of those brackets. Personally I still prefer just one class. I always felt that it was really special when a little team like Warroad, Roseau, or International Falls came to the Cities and tried to knock off one of the big schools.

As the years have passed, there have been many tremendous high school hockey players who have played in the state tournament. I can't start naming names because I would leave out many deserving players. There have been many great ones over the 46 years that I have watched.

The same goes for games, and there have been quite a few that I have worked. But there is one that will always stand out in my mind—

and that was the incredible 1996 game between Duluth and Apple Valley that went into five overtimes.

The goaltending in the game was unbelievable. Those two goalies stopped everything that was thrown at them. The game was so wide open—up and down the ice, back and forth, shot after shot—that no one could score.

The intensity was unbelievable. The pressure and the emotion of the game hit a level almost unreachable. To watch what the kids went through was like nothing I had ever seen before in a high school hockey game—or any game for that matter. It was wide-open hockey and each team had unbelievable chances.

Apple Valley eventually won the game but in my mind, Duluth did score earlier in the game. If there had been instant replay, I think it would have shown it. The referee said that the puck hit the crossbar and did not count. Personally, I think it went in.

Although it wouldn't top the five-overtime game, this past year's four-overtime win by Minnetonka in the second round was one of the all time thrillers, another game that was back and forth with great scoring chances on both sides.

There have been many great teams, players, and coaches throughout the years that represented their communities in such a prideful fashion. The incredible excitement and joy that they experience is hard for us to describe. The winners of the Stanley Cup aren't any more emotional or feel more elation than what these kids experience by winning the State High School Hockey Tournament.

Every year the games seem to get more exciting. At the beginning of the season, each team's goal is to make it to the state tournament. It is an incredible opportunity to see the kids, coaches, students, and fans stream in from all over the state, all with one common focus. I get so caught up in all the passion and excitement. I just love doing it!

• • •

For two years, I did a sports show on WLOL radio in the Twin Cities. Every day, I interviewed a new guest. The interviews lasted just a few minutes, but it was still pretty hectic. At times I had to scramble to get my interviews, but I sure had the opportunity to meet some real characters. I definitely enjoyed it.

One of the most interesting interviews of my life involved a very wealthy man by the name of J.D. McArthur. He was supposedly the richest man in the world at the time, and it had been reported that Mr. McArthur was toying with the idea of buying the New York Yankees from the former owner, Del Webb. I thought he would make for a good interview subject.

I remember traveling out to the end of Singer Island in Florida to get the interview. He was living at a luxurious hotel there. I knew he was going to be a popular interview, so I got there early in the morning, hoping to get in to see him. As I was waiting along with four different magazine writers, I heard Mr. McArthur yell, "Send the hockey guy back!" I didn't know what to expect.

It turned out that we had a great interview. I remember him telling me that he was very serious about buying the Yankees and there was a point when he thought he was going to do it. But then something came along that changed his mind. It was called free agency, a concept that really bothered him. Mr. McArthur told me that he thought it would be a bad thing for the game. He was disturbed about the whole process of players losing loyalty for their teams. He didn't like the idea of them leaving their teams for the big bucks. He was adamant about losing control of the players who had once been under contract. I recall him saying as we visited, "When I buy a politician, they stay bought! You can't say that about a player anymore."

He continued, "So I am going to sit back and watch the games on television and will not put my money into something where players don't want to stay and play for you. I'm not going to do it."

As the interview ended, Mr. McArthur said to me, "Look, kid, you're a good-looking guy, obviously intelligent enough to have your own radio show. Why don't you get out of this hockey business, come down here to Singer Island, and get yourself involved in some real estate? That's where you'll make some real money."

I told him, "I don't think this is a good time. The markets are terrible, the interest rates are high, and nothing is selling." I remember him saying to me, "Now is the time to get in. This is the time when the bright people make their fortune."

And he was right. Shortly after we talked, he bought a condominium building at the end of the island, at a largely reduced price. By the next year he sold them all at triple the price he paid. He sure knew what he was doing. He was one of my favorite interviews.

I interviewed anyone who played any type of sport. I talked to most of the Minnesota Vikings. When we traveled, I tried to get some players in the those cities. I did Mickey Mantle, Muhammad Ali, and seemingly every hockey player known to mankind.

Once, the North Stars went into Philadelphia to play the Flyers. The night before in Boston, I had taken a puck in the face and had broken my nose. Both my eyes were black and my face was really a mess. I wanted to do an interview with Julius Erving of the 76ers, and caught him before their afternoon game.

When I walked in to meet him, he took one look at me and said, "Man, what happened to you?" I told him that I had been hit in the face the night before in Boston. I recall him looking at me in total amazement and saying, "That's why I would never play that game!" Erving was great. We had a really good interview.

I used to go to Twins games often, and during one series I wanted to get an interview with Reggie Jackson of the Oakland A's. I went to their team locker room and was told right up front by their clubhouse man, "Reggie doesn't do interviews." I told the person, "Go tell Reggie

I am a hockey player with the North Stars and I have a radio show and I would like to talk with him." Reggie told him to send me back.

My greatest radio program came as a result of my friendship with Bobby Orr. When he left Boston to go to Chicago, he gave me the story. He called and said, "I have accepted a deal with the Blackhawks and we're having the press conference tomorrow. You can use it today if you'd like." I was the first one to break it on the air.

Another special moment occurred when Francine and I were in Vancouver for a game. The Blackhawks had played there that night. We were having dinner at the Four Seasons Hotel, and Bobby came over to our table and asked if he could join us. He sat down and ordered the most expensive champagne on the menu. I asked him what was going on and he said to us, "I am going to retire tomorrow and I wanted you to know." I will never forget that.

I enjoyed doing the show even during the season. I knew I would not have a career in hockey forever, so I wanted to stay in a regular work routine. My teammates would come to practice in the morning, have lunch, and then go home. I went to work. I wanted to get used to developing strong work habits. Because of my personality, it worked out well for me and I was able to keep busy.

Through my broadcasting career I have covered a wide variety of events. I have done National Hockey League games and CBS television games. I have done *Hockey Night in Canada*, and I have worked the Stanley Cup championship.

During my last season as a player, I would often play a game on Sunday night and then do the *Monday Night Game of the Week* and then meet the team wherever they were on Tuesday. It was quite the grueling time, but I loved broadcasting. Of course, you would never hear of anything like that happening today.

Over the years I have had the opportunity to meet and work with some of the great broadcasters of all time. I did *Hockey Night in*

Canada with Danny Gallivan and Dick Irvin. Both of them were terrific. I worked with Dick Stockton, and maybe the best hockey broadcasters of all time, Al Shaver and Dan Kelly.

Kelly and I did the Stanley Cup championship many years ago. Al Shaver and I have been friends for a long time. And he is surely one of the best radio broadcasters to ever get behind a microphone.

Together, Shaver and Kelly were tremendous. They made you feel like you were at the game with them. They had a way of bringing the intensity and the flow of play right into your living room. They were just unbelievable! They painted a picture for you with words, and you could visualize what was happening on the ice. When you listened to those icons of hockey broadcasting, you were wrapped up in the game as if you were there.

I worked many television games with Dan Kelly during the Stanley Cup playoffs. Dan was one of the greatest TV broadcasters ever. He had a special way of bringing the game to the listeners. I really admired him. Dave Hodge, the host between periods, was another great television person. I worked with Dave on CBC doing *Hockey Night in Canada* games and the Stanley Cup finals on CBS. I have been very fortunate to have had the opportunity to work with such skilled and talented broadcasters and with such class individuals.

ESPN began broadcasting collegiate hockey games in 1980. I worked for them for six years on both their college and NHL telecasts at various times. I also did the NCAA final game between Minnesota Duluth and Bowling Green in Lake Placid. It went into five overtimes. I also broadcasted the 1984 Olympics in Sarajevo for ABC Radio.

When I think back to my days growing up in the Soo and listening to voices like the legendary Foster Hewitt coming to us over the air at night, to later be a part of all that myself almost feels like make-believe. When I listened to Foster Hewitt, I actually felt like I was right there in the arena next to the ice, right in the middle of all the action. He made you feel that way. The play-by-play broadcasters who I worked with were every bit as good as Hewitt.

All of them could paint a picture of the action on ice. They brought you the description of the action with the intensity of what was around them. They brought to you the emotion of the game, the excitement of the fans, and at the same time, painted that picture.

Broadcasting games, I never have tried to emulate anyone I worked with or listened to on the radio or television. Whether I am doing high school, college, the Olympics, or the National Hockey League, I try to tell the listeners what to look for in the game and describe certain things that are occurring. I try to make the game as simple as possible. I am probably the complete opposite from the analysts who are very technical in their commentary. I choose not do that because I don't want to lose the fans. Not everyone watching or listening understands the infinite nuances of the game.

If I talk about the defenseman, I don't say the "D" man on the ice. Some listeners may not have ever laced on a pair of skates or even watched a game before. I say the "crease" and don't refer to it as the "paint." Just making it simple is really important to me.

I remember what Mel Jass told me. It was great advice and it works. I want people to understand what I am saying. I believe it works, so it is still my philosophy today.

When I do high school, as opposed to college, the Olympics, or professional games, I do try to bring across a slightly different kind of message because the level of play is so vastly different. High school hockey is so pure. It is so enjoyable to watch these kids play a three-day tournament and see the kind of enthusiasm they have for the game. The stage during tournament week is huge for them and the manner in which they perform is incredible. There they are on the biggest platform of their life, in front of 19,000-plus in the stands, a huge television and radio audience, and these kids are terrific. It is really something to watch. With their spirited and inspirational play, they can telegraph all of that passion and enthusiasm to everyone watching and listening, and I feel it myself during every single thrill-packed second that I am at the game. It is a wonderful experience.

These young kids put so much into the games that I really do not want either team to lose. And with high school kids, I know I am less critical of what might occur during a game. I am not going to rip a high school player for something that happens. I am much more patient and I protect the high school kids as much as I can. In college games, it is a little different. I don't think about protecting players and I will be much more direct in my analysis and commentary, as well as more technical. The level of play is more sophisticated and the players are more mature.

I also did the University of Minnesota radio in 1991. Naturally, I wanted them to win, but would try to keep my broadcast as unbiased as I could. I also may be more critical of certain things in the game because the level of play is better and players are more developed.

Olympic games and professional games are played by the greatest players in hockey. Those games are easy to do. At those levels, I usually say exactly what I am thinking because the players are so much more skilled and the level of play is so much higher. So I call it like it is.

I have seen some significant changes in the media in the many decades that I have been involved. It is much more competitive and much more negative than it once was. There was a day when the media really cared about the players on their teams and truly wanted them to win. Today the press is much more negative and neutral. Even local media don't keep a rooting interest in the area team's success. Some of the managers, coaches, and players are given a rough time and continually second-guessed.

I have never liked the idea that a writer or radio or television reporter can influence the firing of a coach or manager, or even the trade of a particular player. It's not just about one person losing a job. We are talking about families who are greatly affected by getting uprooted. I don't think it is right, but there are no holds barred in sports today. That's why sports talk shows are so popular.

When I was involved in the game, if a reporter went after one of my coaches or players, I didn't like it. I didn't want them to have any influence on how the fans reacted to a player, or to put pressure on a coach to be fired. I didn't think they had the right to do that. Unfortunately, it still happened despite how I felt about it. These days, it's even worse.

Despite any negative associations with the media, broadcasting has been a great experience for me. I am truly honored by it. Forty-six years of doing the State High School Hockey Tournament has only intensified my enthusiasm for a sport I already loved. I look forward to next year's tournament and hopefully many more. Whether it has been the kids, the collegians, the Olympians, or the professionals, broadcasting has given me the opportunity to tell others about the game that is so enduring to me.

Each year as I start my preparation for the state tournament, my adrenaline starts pumping and my enthusiasm and passion rise to the highest levels. Every year is as exciting as the last. I am extremely blessed to be part of it.

9

Great Arenas

The *Sporting News* has called it "the most storied building in hockey history." I think it was. The Montreal Forum was the home of some of the greatest teams in hockey history. The Canadiens played there from 1926 until 1996, and the arena, the atmosphere, and everything about the setting was amazing. It was hallowed ground, where some of the tremendous Montreal teams won Stanley Cup championships. The ambiance inside was absolutely unbelievable. The fans were incredibly knowledgeable and extremely classy, both in their appearance and in the way they respected the game.

It was a fantastic place to play. The crowd's intensity and passion for hockey and the Montreal Canadiens was unlike any other place I have been. The way the fans were positioned in the arena and their closeness in proximity to the ice made you feel like you were playing the game right in the middle of the crowd. It was magnetic and an experience that stays with you forever; to be there even just one time is to never forget it.

The fans in Montreal are very intelligent. They know the game and understand the action, and the arena was always full of colors.

The fans coming to the Forum looked elegant while attending a hockey game. I think they dressed better than any place connected to hockey. It felt as if you were playing in Paris, it was so wonderful and majestic.

It was not a tough crowd to play in front of compared to some places. For the most part, they were a happy crowd who had an appreciation for good play. There was no doubt they were all in favor of their beloved Canadiens, but they had a profound respect for a good play or an incredible effort from an opponent. It was a prime example of their class. When we came there, it seemed like everyone in the city knew who we were. We could not walk down the streets without someone recognizing us. It was amazing to me.

If the Canadiens fans saw a quality play, they were not afraid to acknowledge it. And they sure saw a lot of quality performances with their own teams for so many years. After all, they had the pure pleasure and enjoyment of seeing some of the greatest players ever to wear the uniform. Players like "Rocket" Richard, Jean Beliveau, Guy Lafleur, and so many others lit up their nights for decades and decades.

When the Canadian national anthem was played before the game and the music and voices of the crowd rose up, it was an overwhelming feeling for me. Everything about the place will be etched in my memory forever—our bench, the Canadiens bench, the locker room, the fans. It was all so passionate and inspirational in every respect. After playing there and being in the historic arena for so many years when I was general manager of the North Stars, I miss every single thing about it.

The Montreal Forum stands empty now and has been that way for many years but every time I hear the name "the Montreal Forum," it still gives me a chill up my back. There is so much history there; it's sad to see it empty. Only two visiting teams ever won the Stanley Cup on the Forum's ice. We did win a Game 7 of a series against them there, and it was unforgettable. Even Tom Lasorda came down to the locker room. He was in town for the Dodgers-Expos baseball series and attended the game that night.

Another of my very favorite places to play was the Chicago Stadium, former home of the Chicago Blackhawks. Chicago Stadium was very loud. If I had to choose one word to describe the crowd there, it'd be "bombastic."

Earlier I mentioned the 1991 All-Star Game, played during the Gulf War. It was one of the most moving nights of my life—and only in Chicago Stadium could there have been that kind of ambience.

Playing in Chicago, it feels like the crowd is all over you. They had the giant organ blaring, and the noise was deafening. The building was essentially a triple-deck box, small by design. I think that accounts for a lot of the noise. And of course there was their famous 3,663-pipe organ, which earned Chicago Stadium its nickname "the Madhouse on Madison."

During the Stanley Cup semifinals in 1971, the Blackhawks scored a series-clinching goal against the New York Rangers, and broadcaster Dan Kelly announced, "I can feel our broadcast booth shaking!" It was such an unbelievable place.

Chicago fans are like no others. They are loud, so passionate for their Blackhawks, and really get into the game. I have been at Chicago Stadium and seen more fights in the crowd than on the ice! Chicago Stadium had a wild, unforgettable atmosphere that was chaotic every time we went there. I absolutely loved playing there. I told Bill Wirtz, the team owner, "You guys are going to give up a goal a game when you move out of here and into your new arena."

Playing in the Boston Garden against the Bruins was another memorable experience. They had the balcony that hung over the ice that was so different from everywhere else. The Garden was such an historic and famous place. It opened in 1928, and because the original intention for the place was as a boxing arena, the fans were very close to the action for both basketball and hockey. The rink was undersized compared to most, and the visiting locker room left a lot to be desired, but it was a really fun place to play. The crowds were boisterous and they loved their Boston Bruins.

I remember one night, we were finishing up the season in Boston and were not going to make the playoffs that year. During the first period, I lost a contact lens. Between periods I went out on the ice on my hands and knees looking for it. One of the Boston fans saw me and hollered out loud enough for me and most of Boston to hear, "Hey, Nanne, why don't you use your playoff money to buy another pair of contacts!" That hurt. Those fans were brutal!

Another place with incredible history was the Maple Leaf Gardens, home of the Toronto Maple Leafs. The Toronto Maple Leafs won 11 Stanley Cups there from 1932 to 1967. Playing there was similar to going downtown to the opera. It was so different than your average hockey game. The people there were always very well dressed. I used to notice the colors in the arena—most of the people wore blue and gray tones—and it was exceptionally quiet in the arena. It was certainly a stark contrast from Chicago Stadium and the noise.

I was amazed at the tremendous differences in the crowds. In Toronto, it sometimes felt like the fans were watching an opera or a play as opposed to a hockey game. But there was a lot of history there despite the serenity of the arena.

When Maple Leaf Gardens was first built in 1931, W.A. Hewitt, sports editor of the *Toronto Star* was hired to be the team's general manager. His son, Foster Hewitt, was hired to run the radio broadcasts, and some two decades later, I was listening to him from Sault Ste. Marie, infatuated with his every word.

Vibrant would be the best word to describe playing in New York at Madison Square Garden. I loved playing in New York, mostly because it is unlike any other city in the world. The Garden in New York was full of great hockey fans and the arena was always buzzing. The fans up high are loud and creative with their criticisms. They were passionate people who came to the games and they knew the game very well. It was always such a competitive atmosphere and the people of New York dearly love their Rangers.

Detroit was the closest National Hockey League city to Sault Ste. Marie, and as I have said, I loved the Detroit Red Wings. They were my team. Detroit played in Olympia Stadium, also called the Detroit Olympia—although some referred to it as "the Old Red Barn"—and it housed my Red Wings from 1927 to 1979.

Like my other favorites, it was an old arena—and the visitors' bench was right in the middle of the crowd. You could be seated arm-to-arm with a spectator—with absolutely no barriers in between. I enjoyed playing there very much, mostly because of my boyhood loyalty to the Red Wings and my hero, Gordie Howe.

The truth is, I enjoyed every place we played; I can't think of an arena that I didn't like. I had the opportunity to see the world playing the game I loved. The arenas were just the icing on the cake.

Even though Buffalo is not one of the original six teams, I have a story about this arena. It was very old, like the others. And when you left the ice between periods, you would have to walk 20 feet through the crowd to get to the locker room.

On one particular night, a gentleman asked if I would come out and take a picture with him and his son after I got dressed. I agreed. A photographer took the picture and I asked what the occasion was. The dad said that we were all Lou Nannes. He and his 11-year-old had the same name! I heard they put the photo in the paper.

Many years later, when Notre Dame was firing coach George O'Leary, my brother called and asked, "Who's this guy using your name at Notre Dame?"

I said, "I don't know, but I'll find out."

I called the Administration Department at Notre Dame, asked for Lou Nanne's office, and got his assistant. It was like the scene from Abbott and Costello's "Who's on First."

"Lou Nanne, please."

"Who's calling?"

"Lou Nanne."

"Yes, it's his office. Who is it?"

"Lou Nanne. Can I speak to him?"

"Who is it?"

This went on for a few seconds until she realized we had the same name. Oddly enough, her name was the same as my assistant's: Terry. I asked if Nanne was from Buffalo but she didn't know. Since he was in a meeting, I left my number and asked to have him return the call. Then he called half an hour later but I was in a meeting. He left a message and asked if I remembered meeting him 27 years earlier. He was the 11-year-old boy. He told me that many times he goes out to fundraisers for Notre Dame and he's asked if he was the hockey player for the North Stars. I told him to take good care of the name.

When our son Michael recently became ill, Nanne called and let us know that he has him in the campus prayer line. I'd say that he has taken care of the name exceptionally well.

As I've underscored, one of my fondest memories was playing for the U.S. team in the USSR. It was 1965 and the Soviet Union wasn't very friendly to the U.S. When we arrived in Moscow we were immediately told what we could and couldn't do. We could not buy, trade, or acquire in any way any religious icons. It was at that moment I knew I had to have one.

I met a man who said he would trade me one in exchange for a Ban-Lon sweater. We would meet in Gorky Park and go from there to the place where we would make the trade. We met in the park and then a policeman came and grabbed him. I said he was a U.S. hockey player and the guy, who spoke English, agreed. The cop let him go and we went to meet his three friends. As I was traveling in the car with the four of them, I thought, *I don't know where I'm going, who I'm with, or what are they up to.* It could have been a disaster. Fortunately, we went to an apartment where I gave them my undershirt, which I said was Ban-Lon, received the icon, and took it back to the hotel. I put it in the slot of my hockey pants in place of the fiber and took it out of the country. I still have it today.

John Mayasich was both a player and the coach of our team. We were playing the Red Army team on an outdoor rink with 10,000 people watching the game. It was an unbelievable setting. It had been very warm outside leading up to the game and the outdoor ice was slushy, with some holes and bare spots on the ice surface.

Our U.S. team had not yet practiced together—we were a collection of players from the United States Hockey League—and most of had been off the ice for two weeks. There was some talk of canceling the game but I intervened. I told John, "Look, we have a chance to stay close. They are one of the best teams in the world and we will have trouble skating with them. But with this ice, it will slow them down. They won't be able to get away from us and it will give us a chance."

I remember three times in the game when the Soviets had breakaways and fell down or lost the puck. The bad ice and the holes worked like a charm. The conditions really played to our advantage. We lost by one goal—the best a U.S. team ever did there.

It was a great thrill for me to have the opportunity to play in all of these arenas all over the United States and Canada, and for that matter, in arenas all over the world. Every one was so different and so special in many different ways.

10

Reflections and Recollections

I have encountered many amazing people in my life and forged so many friendships. These are a few stories of people I have known along the way. Stories that still have the power to make me laugh every time I think of them.

Many years ago, I was involved with former Viking great Alan Page in a commercial for Satoh Tractors. Instead of taking payment in cash, I took a 25-horsepower tractor with a six-foot cut and a backhoe. It was great for cutting the lawn at my farm. I could practically cut the whole yard in two sweeps. When I sold my farm, I took it to Edina.

Francine and I went to Europe on vacation, and when we got home the tractor was gone. My brother Michael was working as a dentist at the time in Eden Prairie and had come over to our house, took my tractor, and drove it 15 miles an hour down the freeway to cut his lawn. To this day, I still cannot believe he did that—and I made him bring it back the same way.

• • •

When I was playing for the North Stars, I became friends with the Minnesota Vikings' great center, Mick Tingelhoff. Mick came out of Nebraska as an undrafted free agent and spent the next 17 years as the starting center for the Vikings. We lived near Mick and his family, so I saw him often.

I loved to tease Mick and used to say to him, "You know, Mick, you football players are so fat and out of shape, it is pathetic. All you do is stand around for a few seconds, snap the ball, and then fall over. I wouldn't even call you guys athletes." I really gave him a hard time about it and I could tell I was getting to him. I didn't let up. I badgered him about the great physical condition of hockey players until he finally had enough.

Our season had ended in April and I had not done a whole lot to stay in shape in the off-season, as I was working. When July came around, the Vikings were getting ready to go to training camp and one night I got a call from Tingelhoff right at dinnertime.

Mick said, "Okay, wiseguy, let's see what kind of shape you're in. Meet me up at Highland Field and we'll see about your conditioning against a *real* athlete." I knew I was in trouble. I had just gotten home from work and had polished off two full plates of spaghetti. I was really stuffed. But how could I turn him down after all the grief I had been giving him?

So we got to the field and began running wind sprints. I was dying. I don't know how I kept that food down, but somehow I did. We went back and forth, back and forth, sprint after sprint. I was in serious trouble but hanging with Mick.

Then Mick stopped and said, "Okay, now we are going to run the track." I'm thinking to myself, *All that food. I'm sick! I'm not going to be able to keep up.*

So we start to run the track and all of a sudden Mick stops, puts his hands on his knees, bends over, and says, "You ———, you are in good shape, aren't you?"

I told him, "This is a piece of cake. I haven't even started yet!" Mick looked at me and said, "Okay, I've had enough." I went home and got really sick. Of course, I never told him.

Mick is a tremendous person. We, along with my North Stars roommate Tom Reid, were the brains and the culprits behind one of the greatest practical jokes ever played on rookie football and hockey players, better known as the "Thanksgiving Turkey Caper."

We got some letterhead from Jerry's Foods, and each year would send a phony letter to all the rookies telling them that they could come into the store and pick up their free Thanksgiving turkeys. So the rookies would get their letters and go to Jerry's Foods for their free turkey. Of course, there was no free turkey and it was always quite embarrassing for them as they tried to walk out of the store without paying for the turkey.

It always worked to perfection, and the joke received some funny media attention. This went on for years. We had a great time with it because we were able to catch a new bunch of fish with every season.

Mick and I always had an enjoyable time together but he really got me good once. The Vikings played at Metropolitan Stadium, which was next to the Met Center in Bloomington. I had a bad shoulder and was unable to play, and our team had left town. I was able to receive treatments from Fred Zamberletti, the Vikings' trainer, in their training room, which was adjacent to the the team's locker room. I would always time my treatments when the Vikings were outdoors practicing because I liked to wreak havoc on their lockers. I used to put baby powder all over their clothes and put a hot balm in their underwear to really mess with them.

One day I was really having a good time messing with their clothes when I heard this incredible noise coming from outside the door. It sounded like a herd of buffalo coming into the room. Coach

Bud Grant had cut the practice short and the team was running into the locker room.

They saw me. They caught me right in the act. Most of them knew I was the culprit but none of them could prove it. Now they knew for sure. Mick, Bill Brown, Bob Lurtsema, Ed White, Jim Marshall, and a bunch of other guys grabbed me, took me in the back, and taped me to the training table. They smeared and painted me with everything they could find in the training room. They put everything they could get their hands on over my body. They got even and then some.

• • •

"Schmutzie" was my defensive partner on our juvenile team, the Algoma Contractors, back in the Soo. When I left for the University of Minnesota, he went to the Junior A St. Catherine's Blackhawks team before continuing his hockey career overseas. At 5'6" he was too short to play defense.

In his later years, he returned to the "Soo" and eventually developed diabetes. My close friend Mike "Zetsa" Scarfone told me that Schmutzie lost both legs. The day he came out of the hospital, he went to Vic's, one of our local watering holes, to see the boys. Everyone was in a good humor. In walked "All Pants" Greco.

Schmutzie's legs were so short that when the waistband of his pants was in the proper place, it looked like the crotch was practically on the ground. That's how he got his nickname. He said to Schmutzie, "Let me see your new legs."

Schmutzie struggled to stand with his new prostheses and finally got up.

All Pants, taking long look at him, says, "For Chrissakes, couldn't you ask for longer ones? You coulda been a six- or even seven-footer. Instead, you look like the rest of the Longarinis: short! At last you had a chance to be taller"

Of course, All Pants was far ahead of his time—it was long before the song "Pants on the Ground."

• • •

The most fun I ever had on television involved former Viking "Benchwarmer" Bob Lurtsema. We did the commercials for Twin City Federal for 10 years. I described it as "the brain and the brawn"—and you could easily tell that I wasn't the latter.

In one commercial, we used the Yellow Pages to demonstrate the strength of TCF. I was supposed to attempt to tear the phone book in half but fail to do so. Bob would take it from me and then tear it himself. The only problem was, I could do it and he couldn't! I would even pre-tear it for him, but the camera lenses could pick it up. Then we thought to use the band saw.

Lurts said it was this low point of his life: hearing the sound of the bandsaw making a fine slice through the book. He tore it and we finished our shoot.

As we were leaving, he begged me to teach him the trick. He said that no doubt someone would ask him to demonstrate his strength at a banquet sometime. I told him he needed to work out harder and longer with more weights. And then I finally relented and showed him how to break the binding and tear with the same motion!

I once invited Bob with me on a horseback riding trip north of Banff. There were 18 hockey players and one football player set to ride 26 miles to Oyster Mountain. We were supposed to have duffel bags that could be easily packed on a horse. Wouldn't you know it, Lurts arrived with two big Samsonite suitcases. Needless to say, we had a hard time keeping them on the horse.

After my playing career was over, I had a nose operation to straighten it out and help my breathing. It felt as if I had 40 feet of gauze in my nose. It wasn't an easy job and I could feel it when I woke. It was brutal.

When I was released from the hospital, Lurts and his wife, Aloise, Francine, and I went to dinner. He asked if it was a tough operation. I lied and said no. I suggested that he fix his nose. After all, no one could understand him. Plus, he would enjoy breathing again, too. "A piece of cake," I told him.

He asked me to set it up with my doctor, which I was delighted to do. The day came for the operation—I waited until I knew he would be awake—and then I called. "How're you feeling?" All I heard were a few hundred swear words and then *"I'm going to kill you."*

When he was out of the hospital and feeling better, we went out to dinner again. Lurts said he bought some land in Burnsville. I said I would buy part and give him my relatively new pontoon as down payment. We agreed. A month later he had my family over for the Fourth of July. When we arrived I suggested we go out for a boat ride.

"Oh sure, you got me good. The boat only goes in reverse," he said. "Let me try it." I started it up, put it in gear, and proceeded to go around the lake—backwards. I am sure it went forward when I sold it to him. He must have screwed it up somehow. Bob has been a terrific foil throughout the years, and we have been fantastic friends.

11

When the Lights Dimmed

A friend recently said to me, "Lou, you are almost 69 years old. You don't have to work. What are you doing?" The answer was easy. I told him, "Yeah, but finance is my game now. This is my hockey game."

The only real difference in what I am doing today compared to what I did for the better part of my life is that I do not lace up a pair of skates every day. There are no buzzers. I don't step onto the ice or into the press box. I don't wear a mouth guard and I don't have to stop a puck with my face any longer. There are no sticks or stitches. The clothes I wear are better, but the thrills are the same. My passion to succeed remains as intense as it ever was.

When I make a sales presentation to a group in an attempt to secure their business, I am in competition with other companies trying to do the same thing. I still feel the pressure and I still experience the highs and lows. Ultimately, if my presentation has been successful and I get the business, it is always a tremendous high. I feel victorious because I have done my job successfully. There aren't any large crowds standing and cheering, and there aren't bright lights and cameras, but internally I feel the same as if they are there with me. And if the decision goes the other way, I am always really disappointed. I will ask myself the same questions I did when I was in the hockey profession. *What could I have done better? How could I have changed my presentation so it would have been more effective? Should I have done anything different?*

All of the self-analysis that I go through has nothing to do with whether or not we have made a lot of money with the deal or missed out on it. Well, maybe a *little*; I suppose we all like to make money. But the underlying issue for me is that it's my game. It's my time under the lights, and I want to perform. And I want to win desperately—just as much as I did in sports.

It is close to the same experience for me that I had as a player, coach, general manager, and president of the Minnesota North Stars. What I do in the world of finance comes with the same passion and emotion that I went through there. It's different in some ways, though, because things are more under my control. When I am performing, I don't have to worry about injuries or others not performing well. It's based on my own individual performance. I enjoy competing with other companies and I enjoy having success. What I do now is just played in a different arena.

The name of my game today is "sell." I enjoy the people I work with every day and I enjoy the business world. The pressures are still there, but not at extreme levels. But this business has many of the same similarities because it takes care of the incredible drive in my personality makeup to win. It is still about winning and I have some of the same kinds of challenges that energize my spirit every day.

Whenever I think or speak about selling, I have to reflect upon my great relationship with my long time mentor and friend, Harvey Mackay. Harvey changed my perspective on everything when it came to business. He personifies the statement "success has no hours." It is no 9-to-5 job; it is nights, weekends, and holidays. Harvey is living proof of that concept. He has given me more valuable insight into selling than anyone.

I first got to know Harvey through the University of Minnesota. He was on the golf team and connected to the M Club. He called me one day and asked to meet. Harvey had started an envelope company and wanted me to come to work for him selling envelopes. I remember saying to him, "Harvey, how can you make any money selling envelopes?"

I will never forget what he told me. He said, "Lou, do you ever stay in hotels? Well, in every hotel there is a shower door, right? Somebody sells those shower doors. It is the same with envelopes. Nobody thinks about them, but sales were made and somebody made money. People use envelopes every day, and once they lick them, they are no good anymore. So they need more. People need envelopes and you can sell them."

So I went to work for Harvey Mackay selling envelopes. He came along at the right time. I had just graduated and was a chemical sales trainee at ADM. The Chicago Blackhawks still owned my rights and wanted me to sign with them. They wanted me to come to training camp, but without a contract, even though we had agreed to terms. I wouldn't go. I knew if training camp went well, I'd get the same contract; if not, they'd try to give me less.

I remember they told me, "Bobby Hull comes to camp without a contract so we are not giving you a contract first."

I told them, "Bobby Hull doesn't have a family or need the money like I do."

We were at a stalemate. So I went to work for Harvey and stayed with him for more than four years while simultaneously playing for the Rochester Mustangs and then the U.S. Olympic Team.

In the beginning, I was frustrated because they had a system in place whereby any contact made by a salesperson gave that salesperson the rights to any future sale at that company. I was making a base of $550 a month, plus commissions. My objective was to get over that hurdle. If I made a sale but someone else at our company had already made a contact there, I lost the commission—even if that salesperson hadn't been there in five years! I didn't like the system, but I had a solution.

I spent a whole week going through the Yellow Pages, contacting more than 1,250 businesses in the Twin Cities and registering myself as the first contact person for all of them. I went to Harvey and told him I had locked up the all of the businesses in the Twin Cities that weren't already covered. Every sale to any of these companies was now mine! He agreed, because that was the system he had in place.

"Lou sets the bar high. He has no fear of failure. If he called on 100 prospects, I honestly believe he thinks he will sell to all 100. He is a ferocious competitor in every respect. He not only wants to run over his competition but will put it in reverse, back up, and run them over again to be sure they are not wiggling."

—HARVEY MACKAY, FORMER BOSS
AND LONGTIME FRIEND

We developed a great relationship and he taught me a great deal. And every time he thought I might sign a professional hockey contract, he gave me another incentive to stay with him. One year he gave me the Pillsbury account. The next year he gave me Honeywell. I was making three times the money I would have been making if I had signed with the Blackhawks.

Harvey always supported me. He never wanted me to leave. He used to tell me, "Lou, the first time you lace up a pair of skates with the pros, you are all done here." Still, when I eventually did sign with the North Stars, he wanted me to stay, but the personal services part of my contract would not allow me to do so.

Harvey has been extremely successful as a businessman and as a best-selling author. I am proud of what I have learned from him and credit him with my abundance of sales knowledge. He has been a terrific mentor and a wonderful friend. I have treasured our friendship over the past five decades.

When I go to a meeting to make a presentation, it is still all about winning. I have to compete. It is who I am. It keeps my juices flowing. In this business I have the opportunity to meet and visit with all kinds of people. I enjoy the interaction and the competition. Most of my business today is done with unions. I want to become involved with their pension funds, make investments for them, and most of all, deliver services to them and all of their employees so they reap the benefits of my efforts.

I was making a presentation to a group some years back and an individual at the meeting was quite skeptical of my background and expertise in the finance business relative to unions. In fact, he asked me point blank, "What do you know about unions?"

There was little question in my mind that his fixation was on my previous career as a hockey player. I'm sure he was thinking, *We have a hockey player coming in here, trying to get our business based on his hockey reputation, and that is not going to cut it with us.* In my mind it was a fair question.

I said in reply, "There is no one in this room that has been connected to unions longer than I have." My response sent shockwaves through the room. Now I had their attention.

I went on. "I am older than all of you and have pensions from AFTRA (American Federation of Television and Radio Artists) and the NHLPA (National Hockey League Players Association). I grew up working in a steel plant in Sault Ste. Marie, Ontario. Each year I worked in a different trade. I have been a media broadcaster for most of my life and I was vice president of the Players Association for more than seven years."

I won them over and solidified for them my expertise in an area of great importance to everyone in the room. I love it when I get asked that question.

When I make a presentation to a group, I usually have about 30 minutes to make my pitch and convince them to do business with me and my company. There may be two or three other presentations the same day, all with the same purpose. I have to be better than my competitors. I have to win them over.

Sometimes my reputation from hockey gives me an advantage. I think it might get me through on a phone call or open a door for me, but that's about it. Past that point, it still comes down to performing and being responsive. The key in our business, like any other sales business, comes down to hard work and performance. We have to meet people, make calls, maintain relationships, and be responsive to our customers' questions and needs.

I have practiced and preached throughout my entire life that there is no excuse for not giving a wholehearted effort in everything you do. There might be someone better than me but they will never outwork me. I have based my entire career—and my life—on that basic concept. I had it in hockey, and I have it in business now. And that's why I have been successful.

When the losses come—and as I mentioned, on occasion they do—I really suffer. I still have not learned how to take defeat. Defeat in business comes not only from losing potential clients after a presentation, but also when I lose clients because we didn't perform for them. That hurts even more because they put their trust in us and we didn't satisfy their goals. When that happens, I am really discouraged because we already had the business and then lost it. And the worst part of the disappointment is that we disappointed our clients. I don't ever want that to happen.

When I look back on it and wonder what we could have done differently, I always hope that it isn't that our competitors outperformed us. Unfortunately, the reality is that sometimes they are better. When that might be the case, I try to look at it the same way that I would have in a hockey game. Once I come to that conclusion, the work begins as I attempt to identify why they are better and what I have to do to turn the tables on them to become the better party.

A successful person always hires the best people he or she may find. I want to hire people who are hungry and who are driven to be successful. I want to work with people who are personable, aggressive, and honest to a fault. I want them to have lots of stamina, a willingness to travel, and a goal to be successful. I want bright self-starters who are well trained in the business.

I can see myself doing this kind of work forever. I don't know what I would do all day if I didn't work. I have to have something to occupy me. And work is fun for me. I really enjoy the challenges that come with it. It is very refreshing for me and I am proud of my knowledge in finance. It stimulates me, motivates me, and challenges me.

When I look back, I am so very thankful that Noel Rahn kept coming to me and saying, "Louie, let me know when you are tired of seeing your name in the papers and want to make some real money." It was this thought put in my head by Noel that provided me with the comfort of knowing that there was another career path for me outside of hockey. And as it turned out, the path has been incredible. I'm glad I took it.

I remember one day I asked Noel, "Well, what exactly do you do?" He said to me, "Louie, all you have to do is get the door open for us and we will take over from there and do all the selling." It sounded pretty good on the surface, but I knew right away that wasn't going to work. I told him, "I'll get the door open, but once we are in, I want to do the selling too because I am not going to be just a name and a face."

Noel told me that he had a job for me if I was ready. At the time we had the conversation, I wasn't quite ready to leave hockey, but I set a preliminary goal that I would leave when I turned 50. I wasn't quite there yet, but it was closing in—as was everything else.

This was about the same time when my obsessions started to become crippling, and the pressures resulted in me going to the Mayo Clinic. It wasn't long after that I realized that it was time to leave. If the Gunds had not kept me on as the president of the North Stars, I would have gone into the financial business even sooner. They were so good to work for, such good friends, that I couldn't leave when they offered me the president's job.

It took about three years before I was ready to leave hockey, and then I cut the cord and started my new career. I talked with Noel and told him that I wanted to be able to sell my services in Canada. He said the holding company had the exclusive rights there. This would have hurt my opportunities considerably so I instead decided to go to work for Piper Capital, which allowed me to work in the United States and Canada. Noel was disappointed, but he understood. I give Noel all the credit for getting me interested. We have been friends for 40 years. This is the reality of how my work in finance began, and I am closing in on almost two decades in money management.

I am doing similar things to what I did in hockey. Only now I try to outsell our competition instead of trying to outplay my opponents. We sell products instead of scoring goals, yet the rewards are much the same. But instead of going up against the few teams playing in the National Hockey League, we are now going up against about 1,000 or more competitors who are money managers.

When I started at Piper Capital, no one was servicing the union pension plans. With my background in unions, I felt it would be a natural for me. It has proven to work very well over the years and the friendships I have made have been wonderful. I am comfortable in this environment because of my background. Going back to my days in Sault Ste. Marie, I had been an oiler, a millwright helper, a bricklayer assistant, and a laborer. I was proud of my background of hard work at the steel plant and was able to use it to my advantage with clients and potential clients in finance. There aren't many people in the business with similar credentials.

> *"Louie is a high-energy person, very emotional and a born salesman."*
>
> —Ed Kohler, former boss and longtime friend

I thoroughly enjoyed Piper Capital and my boss, Ed Kohler. I stayed there from 1991 to 1995. In 1995 Mike Dougherty came to me and offered me the opportunity to come and work for Voyageur Asset Management. I accepted the offer and was allowed to bring eight of my people with me. Mike is a terrific person and a wonderful and caring boss. He gave me and my team the tools to be extremely successful. After two years he made me a minority partner. We continued to grow the business and sold it to RBC Dain in 2000. Our president, John Taft, and I were the only partners who stayed. I am still there today, and now we are called RBC Global Asset Management.

Sometimes I think about my career and compare it to what I was doing as the general manager of the North Stars. I have the same routine when I go to work every day. I used to come into the office and read about what was going on around the league; now I look everywhere to see what is taking place in finance, with the markets, the prospects, and my competitors. I used to call other general managers and make sure I knew about any trades that might be brewing and to get a feel for what was happening with other teams; now I talk with trustees, administrators, and consultants to determine who is interested in making a move and what the tone of the day is in the financial world. I used to sit in the hotel lobby until late at night to be sure I didn't miss anything around draft time; now I use my contacts and observations from all over the country to keep me posted and updated on what is happening. *What kind of products are out there? Are we able to meet needs of our clients? It actually sounds almost the same. What players are available? How do we improve our team to meet our needs?*

> *"I have had over 1,000 people work for me over the years. No one, and I mean no one, works harder than Lou Nanne."*
>
> —MIKE DOUGHERTY, FORMER BOSS AND LONGTIME FRIEND

The juices are flowing and my needs are being met. The ever-changing financial world really gets my adrenaline going. My travels take me all over North America, including Alaska, Florida, Hawaii, and Canada. The competition is fierce, energizing, and enjoyable. At the end of the day, it is another game to win. It makes me feel good to work hard and to be successful.

As I said to Noel Rahn, it was also important for me to do the work and not just to get the door open. The basic premise of paying my own way and being honest about how I earn my money is something my dad taught me early on. I have to do my share; I couldn't work under any other kind of conditions. My dad would say, "Louie, pay your own way. Never let anyone take that away from you." It has stuck with me. I never wanted anyone to think Lou Nanne didn't pay his own way.

This is a business, like many others, in which your confidence level will translate nicely to your success. Having confidence and belief in your product is critical in any sales arena. The ability to perform and have solid relationships with clients is gratifying—especially when you have earned their trust.

My competition puts me up against some of the major financial management firms in the world. It creates the same kind of high for me as what I experienced in hockey. It is the same high, but different people, a different setting. At the end of the day it is still a game—and I want to win with the same intensity and emotion.

It is a magnificent feeling when we are able to secure a commitment from a company after having worked hard to obtain their business. It rivals the joy of reaching the Stanley Cup Finals. Reaping the rewards of hard work is a tremendous feeling. Any time you achieve a goal against great competition, you can say to yourself, "We won out over some very tough competition, so we must be pretty good!"

We never had thousands of competitors in hockey. When I started with the North Stars there were only 12 teams in the National Hockey League. We had to beat 11 of them. At the end of the day the only number that matters is in the win column.

Even though there are some differences, the basic principles remain the same for me every day. Work hard and work hard in a manner in which you operate with honesty and the highest degree of integrity. Commitment and dedication in achieving your goals is the cornerstone of success, but without the honesty, integrity, and credibility, the achievements are meaningless.

When you are in the financial business, you are dealing with people's livelihoods and that of their families. People have put their trust in me and my staff. That is a responsibility that I take very seriously. For me, it is the biggest game of my life. I want to win and I want to win for the people who have entrusted me with their finances. There are not too many things in the working world bigger than that. It is a tremendous responsibility.

The actions of some con artists have created tremendous skepticism in the financial world. They have introduced doubt in a world where trust is essential. Anytime someone entrusts their financial future, they have to have full confidence in the honesty, integrity, and credibility of the person and people who they have invested with. That confidence has been thoroughly shaken in worldwide investing, and it will likely remain unstable for a long time.

As far as I am concerned, when you work with someone, your word must be your bond. There is no room for waffling or compromise. I'll say it again. *Your word must be your bond.*

If you lie, deceive, or break a commitment, how can you ever be trusted again? How will anyone have faith in your word again? Your word is your bond. It must be.

When Norm Green bought the Minnesota North Stars, I was president of the team and closing out my final period in hockey. We had made arrangements to have a team picture taken for a calendar. Norm Green asked about the deal and I told him that Pillsbury was doing the calendar for us to use as a giveaway. They were also going to buy some season tickets and advertising. It was something that had worked out well for us in the past, and for Pillsbury as well. He didn't feel we received enough.

Norm said to me, "I didn't agree to this."

I told him, "You let me negotiate these deals and I agreed to it." He told me to go back to Pillsbury and tell them that he didn't agree to it and that he wants more money.

"No," I told him, "I agreed with them and we made a deal."

He said, "That's okay, just tell them that I don't agree and we want more money."

"No, I won't do that. I made an agreement with them and my word is my bond!"

"Yeah, but you didn't sign anything."

"I don't have to sign anything because my word is my bond! I gave them my word and that is all that has to be done! That's enough.

My word to them is as good as signing a contract and I'm not chang-ing it!"

At that point he told me that he didn't know how long we were going to be able to work together. I told him, "About 45 days, because I already have another job. I am not going back on my word and changing anything with Pillsbury because I agreed to it. When I agree to something, that's it."

People should know that when you make a commitment or agreement, they can take it to the bank. Relationships have to be based on honesty, integrity, and credibility. Without this, a person really does not have much, if anything. I try to live by this philoso-phy every day.

It didn't matter to me if I made a lot of money or very little, but the one thing that I was always going to be sure of is that I earned it. In the hockey business, I needed to win. In the financial world, I want to be successful, too. And by doing that, I need people to be dependent upon me and then I need to produce for them.

When we were in the process of selling the business, I was a minor partner. We had an offer from a company to buy a portion of the business. The part they were interested in was under my purvey— specifically, the equity business. So the new buyers wanted to be sure we were all going to be a part of the deal. They wanted to be sure that we would all stay. While we were on the phone with the board dis-cussing the offer, we received a call from a European firm that also wanted to buy our equity group—and they offered to double my salary if I came on board.

The first thing I asked them was, "What about all the people we had in the Minneapolis office? We have about 100 people involved with the business."

They said to me, "We won't need them. We only want you. That's all we need is you and your asset accounts."

I told them that all of the people in our office depended on me and I could not do that. But they refused to take anyone else. They said they could move all the bond assets to their Houston office to manage.

There was no way that I would ever do something like that, to cause all of those hardworking people to lose their jobs. My co-workers are my team. If I make a sale, we have donuts for the office because we are a team working together. We celebrate our win together.

Now, in the financial business, I am finally able to take some vacations. Francine and I fit in a lot of travel, some of it connected to the business side as well. When I was general manager of the North Stars, I took one vacation in 10 years. I just seemed to work all the time. Now, it's nice to have some vacation travel.

Even so, I still work most of the time. I never seem to have any set hours. I work at night, weekends, whatever it takes. There is a lot to get done. I need to check on things all the time. I am always checking to see if there are searches going on for new managers. I am always checking the industry to be sure I am up-to-date on everything. I am checking to see how our accounts are performing and how the market is doing. I am obsessed with doing the best job I possibly can do. This means I must be on top of every single thing going on.

I have to work to keep the competitive spirit flowing. Without all of this—the scheduling, planning the presentations, researching who we are calling on, setting up travel, calling consultants, prospects, and investment groups—what would I do? When would I be able to play the game? Who would I win against? How would I compete?

As far as my fellow employees go, they are fantastic. I want to assist them in every way possible in order to be successful. I will fight their battles for them, be loyal to them, and support them in any way I can. I encourage them to be successful and try to provide guidance in order to give them the best chance to win at the same game I am playing. It's fun, challenging, and I think a terrific opportunity for me to get out of life what I need in order to remain busy and feel worthy.

I do not hire untried, untrained people. I hire superstars so they will excel quickly. I want them to be trained somewhere else so we can go and convince them to come and work for us and be immediately productive. When the times are tough, it is important to continue to bring in revenue. It is the most important time to instill trust. Good employees develop strong personal relationships. Clients need to know that you care about them. They need to know that you will keep them abreast of what is happening in the world of investments, and particularly with their individual portfolios.

I want employees who will go the extra mile for their clients. It's the way I would want to be treated by someone managing my own accounts. This involves spending time with them, advising them, and doing everything possible to cement the relationship, while enhancing it as well. Harvey Mackay taught me the importance of relationships and how critical contact with organizations and clients is.

"Lou is very honest and straightforward. You always know where you stand with him. He is an extremely hard worker and will always give everything he has to the job. I have worked for Lou for over 20 years and he has been a great boss. He is sensitive, caring, and very considerate of others."

—Terry Magnuson,
executive assistant

I want employees who will be with us for the long haul. I don't want a transient staff that will be gone soon after they are hired. When I am interviewing people for a job with us, I want to get a feel about them. *Are they going to work well with clients and fit in well with us? What kind of personality do they have? Are they caring and sensitive? Do they seem to have empathy?* All this and much more goes into whether I think they will be a great fit in our organization.

I also want to be convinced they have an extremely high work ethic. I like people who want to be successful. I have often heard in the industry that it is a good thing to have salespeople who have high mortgages. The theory is that a person will then work hard to pay for their mortgage. I don't buy into that. I want people who are driven to be successful. I want them to enjoy the finer things in life because they are a success. But it isn't all about work. First, you need to be a success at home. Once that is taken care of, then comes success in business. It would be hard on an individual to focus properly if he or she has other concerns on the home front.

Sometimes it is hard for me to remember that I can't expect the same from people who work for me that I expect from myself. I said before, I will not be outworked. There might have been a better player on the ice than me, but he never outworked me. It would be a little unfair to expect the same from my staff that I expect from myself. If it is a given that I will not be outworked, then how could I expect someone to give more effort than I do?

Instead, I measure their performance against industry standards. We have a good handle on what the industry level of success is, and we utilize it as a standard of measurement

The business world rewards great effort and hard work. Good things happen to people who work hard. To be successful, you have to have a big appetite and work to satisfy it, not here and there, not a few days a week, but every single day. There are no set hours in the business world. And when a person really enjoys their work, it no longer is a job. Time spent becomes irrelevant.

When I was playing bantam hockey in Sault Ste. Marie, we had Marty Pavelich of the Detroit Red Wings as the speaker for our year-end hockey banquet. I will never forget what he said to the team. He told us to always watch someone who is better than you. If you are a bantam player, watch the midgets. If you are a midget player, watch the juveniles. If you are a junior player, watch the senior team. If you are a college player or junior, watch the professionals. You always watch someone better than you and then try to emulate them. And by doing this, you will become a better player because you will improve your play.

He went on to tell us there are always times when you can improve when you least expect it. For example, walking to school, if you see a can on the street, practice kicking it from one foot to the other, back and forth, front foot to back foot, because in a game that's what you do with the puck. The more you do this and practice it, the better you will be at moving the puck around with your skates. The more proficient that you get at something simple like this, the better player you will be.

The message he left with us was, "Don't waste time. There is always something you can be doing to improve yourself."

In my mind, it is the same in business. Look at the salespeople that are better than you. What are they doing that makes them so successful? How do they work? What makes them so special? Why do others always want to be around them, picking their brain? What are they doing that you are not doing? How can I change my work habits to be as successful? It works! Watch someone who does what you do and utilize their experience and expertise to make you better at what you do.

I have had many mentors in my life, people who have helped me understand the big picture and how to be successful in my careers. I have never been afraid to ask questions and learn as much I could. I question, question, question because I want to know. My mentors have answered those questions for me and helped me in my career. *How would you go about doing this? What advice would you give about that? Why do you do it that way?* It's kicking that can down the street from foot to foot.

If I see someone who is really good or exceptionally proficient at something, I want to know why and I ask them. Some people go through life and never inquire about anything. They miss out on so much.

I love to watch people who are successful. I am intrigued by their success. I am mesmerized by it and I want to know why and how. It's interesting to see the changes in baseball management today. Sharp businesspeople are put in top positions and surround themselves with talented individuals from the baseball world. Theo Epstein of the Boston Red Sox is a perfect example.

Today there are a number of successful sports operations that are run by executives who never played the sport. The sports world is big business in this era, with lots of dollars on the line. A person needs to be knowledgeable about the business aspect of their work. You can hire people to run the baseball or football side of the operation, but it's important to have business sense in order to run the overall operation.

What drives me is the incredible will within me to succeed. Maybe some of that is insecurity, I don't know for sure. It might be that I cannot stand the remote possibility of failure. Maybe that's why I have the energy and willingness to work as long and hard as I can.

There was a television broadcaster in Sault Ste. Marie by the name of Russ Ramsay, and he would have all the winning teams in the area on his program. One day he said to me, "Lou Nanne, you are here all the time. It seems that you are on every winning team we have on the show. Hockey, baseball, softball, it doesn't matter, you are always here!" I got used to being with and around successful teammates and people, and I like it.

Maybe it's having some doubt or insecurity that drives me like it does because I know I cannot accept failure. Yet, if this is a possibility, it does not affect me in how I do my work. I am extremely secure in my way of doing business. I have the utmost confidence in my ability to perform my job.

I never have had an issue or problem in giving my opinion or doing certain things a certain way. Once I make up my mind about what I am going to do, I do it. I would never have made as many trades in hockey without that trait. Don't get me wrong—I will question things and have doubts before moving ahead, but once I make my decision, it's full speed ahead and I am ready and willing to face the consequences.

In business, I am constantly analyzing how we do things. I know I can always be better, and that's what I strive for every day of the year. I want to be better because if I am, I will win more often.

Just the other day, I was thinking about our 1987–88 team and told someone that I made a critical mistake with that particular squad. I said we needed more speed on that team and at the time, I didn't recognize that. We had lost too much speed from the previous years, and I had not replaced it. Now, some 20 years later. I know I can't go back in time and find the speed. It's too late. But I never stop analyzing. Look what happened with that team. Why didn't I do something about the speed? Why wasn't I aware of it at the time?

I want to learn. I want to learn from others. I want to know what everyone else knows. I am driven by wanting to know what other people know that I don't know. I look at all of the people that I have known in my life who have been successful and I have such an incredible amount of admiration for each of them. Each has his own special skills. They have been my mentors and have assisted me along the way. I have been guided by them and have watched and learned from them.

Throughout my years in business and in life, I have learned a lot that has contributed to my success. Here are a few tips that have been successful for me. These are personal experiences and lessons from my time with Harvey Mackay. I want to share them with you.

What It Takes to Be Successful

1. There is a saying that the problem with opportunity is that it comes disguised as hard work. There is another: The greatest mistake you can make is to be continually fearing that you will make one. That's why the great players always want the ball in critical situations. Success is overcoming those fears.

2. When you feel confident, you act confidently. As a salesperson, I go in believing that I am there to improve their portfolio and they should be doing business with me. If you don't believe, the prospect will notice.

3. Never permit failure to become a habit. Have the proper attitude. One's attitude determines one's altitude. It is one of the most significant ingredients to success or failure.

4. Be a self-starter. The pep talks, the push, and the inspiration must come from within to keep you going, hour after hour and day after day. I would follow an envelope truck belonging to one of my competitors and see who their best customers were. Then I'd call on them.

5. Be creative and flexible. Think outside the lines. Figure out ways to make it work and be better. There is always a better way to do something. Find it, and then find a way that's even better.

6. Be a team player. Let others know that they can depend on you and that you can depend on them. You don't have to spend long hours together outside of the office, but you must pull and work together.

7. Have great passion to succeed. This is the prime ingredient that moves one from mediocrity to excellence.

8. Always make sure you are underpaid. It sounds illogical, but the underpaid people make the most money. Make sure you can never be compensated for your worth.

9. Be a good listener. You can make more intelligent decisions with more information.

10. Improve your communication skills. Take speech and interpersonal relations training. Be the type of person others want to be around.

11. Establish informal mentorships by watching successful people's actions, and try to utilize their skills within your own abilities.

12. Show people that you care. Compliment good work and thank those who deserve to be thanked.

Just as crucial are networking skills. In my business, the personal relationship is everything. You never know when an important contact will come into your life. With well-honed networking skills, you can always be at the ready.

1. Remember the people you meet and what they do. Use index cards to organize information on contacts.

2. Develop a strategy for remembering names and important facts about them.

3. Ask friends about acquaintances who may be helpful.

4. Keep abreast of relevant business journals, newspapers, and magazines.

5. Be observant. When you enter someone's office, take a mental inventory. Some items may be good conversational material.

Matching Skills with Openings Available:

1. Try to define who you are, what you want, in terms of the work you would like to do:
- Buy into the team concept at work
- Identify with the company
- Commitment and performance are key
- Remember that there are many different paths to success, not one right path

2. People with different personalities, different approaches, and different values succeed not because one set of values or practices is superior but because their practices are genuine.

Company Particulars

1. Research the company before you step in the room.

2. If you have friends who are familiar with the company, ask them questions about it and get a better understanding of the operation.

3. Find out who your competitors are—and get information about their strengths and weaknesses.

And finally, something I read and loved.

I do not choose to be a common man. It is my right to be uncommon—if I can. I seek opportunity, not security. I do not wish to be kept a citizen, humbled and dulled by having the state look after me. I want to take the calculated risk; to dream and to build, to fail and to succeed. I refuse to barter incentives for a dole. I prefer the challenges of life to the guaranteed existence; the thrill of fulfillment to the stale calm of utopia. I will not trade freedom for benefice nor my dignity for a handout. I will never cower before any master nor bend to any threat. It is my heritage to stand erect, proud, and unafraid; to think for myself, enjoy the benefits of my creations, and to face the world boldly and say, this I have done. All this is what it means to be an American.

—*Dean Alfange*

Every day is another opportunity to learn something new. I am absolutely driven to find it and use it to improve my life. It is what I am all about.

I sincerely hope that my goals, dreams, accomplishments, and philosophy on business and life is a help to others who are driven to be successful. I hope there is a full appreciation and understanding of the guiding principles of honesty, integrity, and credibility and the importance of each toward being a success with family, business, and life. If it is, and others are to be guided by them as I have been, then I cannot ask for anything more.

12

Greatest Loves
and Passions

I can't fix anything. I am absolutely no good around the house. The other day Francine told me that she had to pick up a certain type of filter for the furnace. I didn't even know there was such a part. I know we have a furnace, I'm just not sure where it is.

Francine runs the house. She fixes everything that needs fixing and keeps it in great shape. But she is much more than the handyman around the house; she is the cornerstone of our family. I don't know how I would have survived without her. And I have enjoyed every minute of my life having had the blessing to be with her over all these years.

Once I was on a television program one night after a particularly rough game where I had been banged around pretty good. When I got home, Francine said to me, "Lou, you should have seen how your face looked on TV. It was swollen and black and blue. How could you go on TV looking like that?"

I countered with, "Yeah, but I got you a Black & Decker power drill."

We have been with each other for more than five decades, and this year we will celebrate our 48th anniversary of marriage. We first started going together in Sault Ste. Marie when I was 14 and she was 12. Her family moved from Montreal to the Soo, right around the corner from us. When we first met, she could barely speak English, only French. Her mother acted as an interpreter for us when I asked her to go to a high school dance with me.

We were engaged when I was 20 and married when I was 21 and she was 19. I was going to the University of Minnesota at the time, playing hockey for John Mariucci. During the summer, I worked at the Algoma Steel Plant. Every opportunity I could, I asked for an overtime shift. We went 7–3, 3–11, or 11–7. After continually getting these extra shifts, I wondered why Mac the Millwright didn't ask for any. He said, "Lou, I came into this world with no money and I'm going out the same way with no money. You can have it all."

Francine needed a visa to come to the United States to work and she needed a sponsor. We had little money and our plan was for her to come to Minneapolis and get a job.

It turned out I actually didn't get any advice or counsel from John about how to get a sponsor for Francine because all I had to do was ask about the process and it was taken care of immediately. His response was, "I will be her sponsor." We never have forgotten John's thoughtfulness and caring for our needs at the time. It was really special for us.

Francine was able to find a job and went to work for Korhumel Steel. She worked for eight months and quit when she became pregnant. I knew I'd better graduate on time if we wanted to eat.

We have had a wonderful life together. I knew right away that she was going to be a wonderful mother to our children and she has been just that. Francine is one of 11 children in her family. Soon after we met, I watched her with her younger siblings and noticed how great she was around kids.

We enjoy golfing together, movies, traveling, and attending hockey games. She has a passionate interest in hockey like I do. As my life has moved along in many various stages, she has always been there for me. I have always asked her opinion and value what she thinks.

When I was the general manager of the North Stars, I always wanted to know what she thought of the moves we made, how we played, and so on. I felt her perspective represented a fan's thinking. Francine knows the game and understands it. Sometimes when I am traveling and miss a Wild game or one of the grandkids' games, she always fills me in and keeps me updated.

> *"Living with Lou has been a wonderful adventure. He is an extremely interesting person. He is a deeply caring and passionate person with a tremendous love for his family."*
>
> —FRANCINE NANNE

Whenever I was out of town, she would still go to the games. Since I have always traveled a great deal in the jobs I have had, she has often been alone. She has always understood what my work has entailed and takes care of everything on the home front.

I have always marveled at how handy she is around the house; it is amazing to me. When we bought our first house, we paid $18,500 for it. It was in good shape but needed to be painted. Francine came to me and said, "Lou, we have to paint the living room." I recall telling her, "I can't paint a lick. I don't know how to paint." She said to me, "You are painting!"

The next thing I knew, I had a paintbrush in my hand and I was painting. Francine looked over at my work and says, "You are terrible!"

I said, "I know, I told you that!"

"Okay," she said, "You can quit, but you're not going anywhere. You can sit there and watch me paint." So I just sat there and watched her paint. She painted the entire living room—and, I might add, did a great job. I provided the pizza.

Whenever I was asked to be on a radio or television show, they always gave a gift for the appearance. I usually could pick from several items and I always brought home things for Francine like drills, hammer sets, tools—whatever she needed. They wouldn't have done me any good but she sure made good use of everything.

I have loved our life together. The most important thing we have in common is our love for each other and our children and grand-children. We are a very close family, and without them we would have very little. There is nothing quite as special for us as being all together.

I have a deep appreciation for family. My parents taught me the importance of that. My memories of Mom baking on the weekends until early morning and Dad telling me that all our relatives were going to be at our wedding because they will be the ones at your funeral stick with me.

We have four incredible children and 11 grandchildren. They are all wonderful, thoughtful individuals. Our oldest daughter is Michelle. She is a whirlwind, and if she wanted to, she could have been a marvelous salesperson. She is really people-oriented and driven. She used to be a flight attendant and always had things under control. She has been an exceptional mom.

Next in line are our twin boys, Michael and Marc. They are 11½ months younger than Michelle. Michael is a dentist and Marc is in the commercial real estate business. They have been wonderful sons to us and are very close as twin brothers and identical in appearance. They are great parents, too, as all of our children are.

Marty is our youngest by three years. He has his own insurance business. He is also a terrific son and is the one who scored the winning goal for Edina in 1984 to win the State High School Hockey Championship while I was broadcasting. What a great thrill that was! He played professional hockey until a neck injury cut his career short. In fact, our scouts had just asked me to acquire him because they thought he could make our team.

All of our kids are close, which makes Francine and me very proud. When I think about my life's great loves and passions, I knew that the only place to begin was with Francine and the kids. Without them, I would have nothing. Many years ago, I found out about what was important in life. Michael was severely injured in a motorcycle accident. For 72 hours, we did not know whether he was going to live or die. During that time, I can recall thinking many times that I would give up every single thing that I had, just to have Michael live.

I kept thinking, *God, why didn't you let this happen to me? I am 41 years old, take me instead of Michael.* I would have given up anything to have Michael live. None of it meant anything to me in the scope of what was happening to our family.

When Michael was 18, we were driving as a family to Sault Ste. Marie. Francine and I were about to embark on a trip to Monaco and Nice, so the kids were staying with family. We planned to spend some time with the Fletchers and Greens on Norm's private yacht and then spend several days in Paris.

On the way to the Soo, we were stopped at a stop sign when a great big Harley Davidson motorcycle pulled up alongside of us. Michael, who was sitting next to me, said, "Dad, I really want one of those."

I told him, "You will not have one of those as long as you are living in our house." I told him that one of my brother's best friends was killed in a motorcycle accident.

We spent about a week on the yacht and then went out to dinner in Nice with Cliff Fletcher and his wife, walked some on the beach, and went back to the hotel to go to bed. The next day we were going to Paris.

I couldn't sleep. I was tossing and turning all night long. Francine finally said, "What's the matter with you? You have been awake all night."

I told her, "I know. I can't sleep. I really don't want to go to Paris. I wish we were going home." Just as I said that the phone rang in our room. It was my sister on the phone. "Louie," she said, "You have to come home right away. Michael has been in an accident. He's okay but you have to get here as soon as possible."

So we got up, got dressed, and caught a flight from Nice to Paris and then flew to Montreal, Toronto, and finally to Sault Ste. Marie. It was miserable—the longest 20 hours of our lives. We ate no food and had no drinks, only water. We could not even get off the plane in Montreal as they were only there to gas up the plane. I told the crew I had to get off to make a phone call. Once they learned of our situation, they agreed to let me off the plane.

There had been a man sitting near us on the plane who told us that he had lost three of his children over the years due to accidents. I could never understand how he survived the grief. I made the call and found out that Michael was still alive, but that he had been severely injured. Michael was riding a motorcycle and the boy who hit him was also on a motorcycle. The boy had been passing a truck when they collided. The other boy was wearing a helmet but was killed in the accident; Michael had not been wearing a helmet, but he was still alive—barely.

He was in a coma. We were told if he made it through the next 72 hours, he would have a chance to live. When the accident happened, my son Marc, Michael's twin, felt immediately there was something wrong. He had been staying in our family cabin, and one of the cabins had been rented out by my aunt to a nurse. He went to find her and brought her to the scene of the accident.

The crash had been severe and the ambulance crew didn't take care of Michael's bleeding at the scene. Fortunately, by bringing the nurse, Marc saved Michael's life. She was able to get the bleeding under control otherwise Michael would have died at the scene. She put a tourniquet on him and saved his life.

He had three blood transfusions after he got to the hospital and was in extremely serious condition. He was in a coma, had a broken femur, lost his spleen, and had a damaged shoulder and severe head trauma. When Francine and I finally got to the hospital we were shocked at his appearance. Because of all the trauma he was holding a lot of water, so he looked huge.

All we could do was wait. As we waited, we were all dying inside. Once the 72 hours passed and we thought he was going to be okay, the doctor came in and told us that gangrene had set in in his leg and we had to make a decision. He told us, "You are going to have to take his leg or take a chance on his life."

I called Dr. Harvey O'Phelan in Minneapolis. I told him what had happened and he consulted with Michael's doctor. Dr. O'Phelan then advised me that in his opinion Dr. Fife was right and we probably would need to have Michael's leg removed. So we made the decision to do that.

Once the leg was removed, he had to be transported to London, Ontario, where the trauma center is known as the best in Canada. Gordon Gund sent a plane for us to meet Michael there. Michael's entire leg had been amputated and now we had more waiting. Another 12 hours before we knew for sure if he would live or die.

I can remember lying on the floor, trying to get some sleep. The next morning, the medical staff advised us that the gangrene had not spread. They had gotten it in time. Michael remained unconscious for a week. It was incredibly difficult to see his twin brother, Marc, watch everything that went on. If he felt something wasn't right, he would immediately call for a nurse. But miraculously, Michael was alive. That was all that mattered.

We knew we were going to be there for a while so we rented an apartment in London. After a week had passed, Michael came out of the coma. He stayed another three weeks to rehabilitate. When Michael was ready to travel, he was taken to the University of Minnesota Hospital. We were fortunate that Twin Cities businessman Bob Short had his private plane bring us back home. We always have appreciated that gesture as well as Gordon Gund's thoughtfulness to fly us to London, Ontario.

The most difficult thing that we have ever had to do was to tell Michael that his leg had to be removed. One of the things I know helped me came from the time I spent in hospitals on a USO tour. After a Sunday football game, while playing for the North Stars, we had Minnesota Vikings players Fran Tarkenton, Mick Tingelhoff, and Jim Marshall and their wives over to our house for dinner. Jim Marshall told me about his USO tour to Hawaii to see the troops. I told him I wanted to do that and asked him how to go about it. I wanted to visit the troops in Vietnam.

Shortly after, I contacted the USO. They told me, "Well, we have never sent a hockey player on a tour before."

I said, "You have one now."

They told me they needed a group to go. "I'll get a group together."

They told me they needed a group leader. I said, "I'll be the group leader."

They told me I needed permission from the NHL. I said, "I'll get permission from the league." And I did.

We were sent on a hospital tour through Japan, the Philippines, Okinawa, and Guam. We saw guys who had just been flown in to the hospital. They were really badly hurt. Some had their legs blown off, their arms, and stomachs blown out. Most of them were in really bad condition. Some were literally burned from head to toe. I will never forget going through those hospitals and seeing those kids.

It helped me personally after Michael's accident. Some of those kids were so brave. They had such incredible attitudes. I remember one young man who had just lost his leg say to me, "When I get home, I am going to ski again." Others told me what they planned to do. I couldn't believe it, the courage they had expressed. It was such an inspiration for me. The following year I had the opportunity to go to Vietnam. Those experiences really got me in the right frame of mind to talk with Michael about what had happened to him.

I said to him, "Michael, I know losing your leg is terrible, but I have to tell you something that I remember. When I was in Japan and the Philippines during the Vietnam War, I was in the hospitals and I saw young men in much worse condition than you. They told me how they were going to ski and play golf again. You are going to be okay, Michael. If they can do it, you can do it."

I saw these young men show their determination in the face of injury. It helped me immensely when that injury hit home, and I know it helped Michael.

A few months later, Gordon Gund called me and said, "Louie, take Michael to Aspen skiing. If I can ski blind, he can ski with one leg." He set us up with a trainer and by the fourth day, Michael was skiing the black runs. He was a good skier before the accident and he was going to be good again.

Later, Michael played golf with Arnold Palmer at a Courage Center event and shot the best nine holes of his life. It was amazing and so wonderful. He has handled his situation as well as anyone could have handled such a traumatic event in his life. When he first came out of the hospital I told him, "I'll get you a handicapped sticker for your car."

Michael looked at me and said, "I'm not handicapped."

I said, "I know you're not but I like to park close, so you're getting one!"

He has done well in his life since the accident. Today, he is the dentist for the Minnesota Wild hockey team. But more important, Michael's accident has made a difference in our family. It has made us all aware of the fragility of life. How lucky we were that Michael lived. Now, however, he is going through another tough time, battling a brain tumor. Michael is so strong willed and positive, we all are confident in his ability to battle it.

In just a split second, something can happen that can change your life forever. It made us more aware of what is really important in our lives. It made us appreciate what we have and treasure our family and our value systems. All that is really important in life is your family; your parents and your kids, and of course the marvelous grandchildren.

I tell my grandchildren all the time, "If I knew you guys were going to be so much fun, I would have just had grandchildren!"

• • •

Even though I am not involved in playing or managing hockey any longer, I still have great passion for the game—indeed, for most sports. When Dan Barreiro and I do the radio show on KFAN in the Twin Cities every week, we talk about all kinds of things that are going on in sports.

Recently a friend asked me, "Louie, how do you keep up with sports from the Wild to Gopher football, basketball, the women's Olympic hockey team, and all the other things you talk about?" Well, I read. I read a lot. I read several newspapers. I read on the Internet. I watch all the news channels, all the sports channels, and I listen. Sports are of interest to me so I follow everything. It's fun for me, and also relaxing.

Golf is another of my great passions in life. I have played golf courses all over the world and I absolutely love the game. I am not obsessed to shoot in the 70s; I just want to go out and have fun. Sure, I like to beat the guys I am playing with, but mostly I really enjoy being out on the links.

My biggest thing on the golf course is to play fast. Someone recently asked me how my round was. My reply was, "Two hours and 10 minutes." If I can play a fast round of golf, I am happy. There is a belief at my club that my ambition in life is to finish with the foursome in front of me. I love being outside. I love playing all kinds of different courses and I truly enjoy the game. But I can't answer the question that once was asked of me: "Why do you love to play, but can't wait to get off the course?"

It doesn't matter how long you've played; in golf, every time you take a swing it's a challenge. Most of the time, I shoot around 90 so I am reasonably competitive. I'm happy with that. But if I shot 92 but we played in two hours and 10 minutes, I would be content.

Playing golf is usually not supposed to be an adventure where your life is in danger. However one day mine was—along with my son Marty and several other friends on a golf outing in 2001 to Giants Ridge in Northern Minnesota. We left from Wayzata Bay in the Twin Cities on Rick Born's float plane. It was about three weeks after 9/11. I was sitting in the copilot seat as we headed out, and it wasn't too long before I was in desperation trying to get out of the seat.

When we left the Twin Cities, we had blue skies, but as we got closer to our destination we entered cloud cover with a very low ceiling. The conditions were severe enough that I suggested we alter our course and head somewhere else to play. Our pilot would hear none of that talk. I recall him saying to me, "You know hockey, I know flying. I have been flying these planes for 25 years in the bush of Alaska. This is not a problem."

A short time later we came out of the clouds and discovered that the ceiling had been so low that we were barely above the water. Now I knew we were in trouble. The plane and all seven of us in it crashed into the dock at our destination. The plane skidded off and we hit another before we came to a stop in the water, in a tilted position. I never had given any thought during the landing that the crash might kill all of us but now I wasn't so sure. Everyone seemed to be okay as they got off the plane, but I was trapped—I couldn't get my seat belt loose. Finally, the pilot was able to get me loose, and I got off the plane to safety.

People seemed to appear from all over to see the wreckage and make sure we were all right. Thankfully, we were. And so were our golf clubs. So what would any group of avid golfers do after getting into a plane crash? Go play golf, right? So we did.

I remember calling Francine before we teed off to tell her what happened. I said to her, "Francine, I want you to know what happened because you are going to hear it on the news. We are all okay, but we were in a plane crash. Now we are going to play golf."

She got mad at me and said, "Why do you say crazy things to me? Why would you say something like that about being in a plane crash?"

We later learned that approximately 95 percent of people who crash in float planes are killed. We were all very lucky!

Even with the plane crash as a part of my golfing resume, I usually play once or twice a week during summer, and I will play with anyone. It doesn't matter who I am with, I just enjoy the game. I also really like to watch golf and have had the opportunity to watch tournaments all over the world. I always marvel at the professional players and the incredible golf shots they make. It is unbelievable how they can control the ball and play under the tremendous pressure of competition. Me, I just want to play in two hours and 10 minutes.

One sport that I don't enjoy is swimming in the ocean. The last time I tried it, I almost drowned. In August of 1985, when I was general manager of the North Stars, Gordon Gund invited Francine and me and Hugh Scott and his wife to their home in Nantucket. While we were there, Gordon suggested we go with him to Tuckernuck Island to do some clamming. When we got there, it was decided that we would go swimming. I didn't want to go. In fact, I thought they were nuts. Hugh would stay in the water near Gordon, who was blind, but I was thinking, "What about me?" Hugh had been on the college swim team; I just swim to cool off.

Gordon told me I would be fine, and that if I swam with the current I would always be headed for land. I didn't listen very well and soon found myself out in the ocean and in deep trouble. I jumped in and immediately started swimming ferociously, with no bearings on where I was headed. I was swimming against the current and getting farther and farther from shore. Gordon and Hugh were about 50 yards away from me and didn't know what I was doing.

Soon I was exhausted. I realized I was going the wrong direction. Past experience taught me I could not tread water without sinking like a rock, so I yelled twice for help—to no avail. I thought, *I am going down. I am going to drown right here on the top of the* Andrea Doria. *This is where my life will end.*

Then I started to talk to myself. I said, "I am a professional athlete and have had to rise to the occasion many times." I began to pull myself together. I remembered what Gordon had said about the current and I started slowly swimming in the right direction to get to shore. With not an ounce of energy left, I remember my face hitting the sand. I lay there in the sand for what seemed like an eternity. I could not move. I had nothing left and then Gordon stepped on me. He asked Hugh, "What's that?"

"It's me," I managed. Not knowing my condition, Gordon suggested a drink and then another swim. I told him that I almost drowned and that I would never go swimming in the ocean again for the rest of my life!

Ironically, in 2006 I rented a villa for George Gund, Glen Sather, Doug Risebrough, Jack Sperling, Jerry Schwalbach, and our wives during the Olympics in Torino, Italy. It turned out the place was owned by the Doria family! I was much happier staying at their place in Italy than at their other place in the Atlantic Ocean. Swimming I can do without in my life.

I'm not sure if my knee will ever be good enough for me to someday play old-timer's hockey. I have not played since I had a knee replacement and I sorely miss the games with the North Stars alumni. I also loved competing in their exhibition games—and believe me, we didn't want to lose those, either.

"Louie is as genuine a person as you will find anywhere. He has a heart as big as the whole world. There is nothing he wouldn't do for his family and friends."

—Jerry Schwalbach, longtime friend

I don't want to see young kids or my grandkids have the same intensity that I have. I know what it can do to a person, and I don't think it is a good thing. I want them to be able to reach their own level of intensity and not to have a parent or a coach tell them how they are supposed to feel. Kids need to have fun and enjoy the game for what it is. I really enjoy watching kids play hockey and frankly, I get excited about every game I am watching. It is in my blood and will always be there. It is such a great game and so incredible to be a part of and watch.

My passion for the game is never-ending. Every part of it excites me but there are some things that really bother me. Fighting in the National Hockey League is one of them. I don't have a big problem with two guys getting involved in a scuffle and dropping their gloves to go at it. But I do have a real issue when a player makes a great check on someone, a hit within the rules, and then someone else comes along and starts a fight because of it.

Contact is obviously one of the most important parts of the game. It sells tickets and makes the games exciting to watch. If the league continues to allow the fighting after a good body-check, some players will intimidate those who play within the rules and we would lose the contact part of the game. Pretty soon the good body-checkers will quit doing what they do because they will be facing a fight soon after. That's wrong, and it will seriously hurt our sport.

There was a time years back when some of the greatest fighters and tough guys on the ice were also some of the game's greatest players. Players like Gordie Howe of the Detroit Red Wings and John Ferguson of the Montreal Canadiens were really tough, but their all-around play was impeccable. Back then, rosters were not large enough to carry a player just for the purpose of fighting. You simply had to be a good player. In the modern game, with the expansion of the rosters, there are more guys who are only known to be enforcers, so to speak. When I managed the North Stars, I had a name for those guys; I called them "equalizers." Of course, on the other teams, I called them "goons." The fact is, there are a number of players who would not even be in professional hockey today if fighting was banned.

Today, there is a fear that the game will not be as attractive if fighting isn't allowed. I don't agree. People would come to the games. People who stay away because of the violence may decide to come. Fighting is not necessary to make the game of hockey exciting. You can have it in the game but I believe it should be a spontaneous event. Consider the Stanley Cup playoffs and the Olympic Games. Rarely do you ever see a fight at those games—and they showcase the greatest hockey in the world. The game of hockey is fast, aggressive, and exciting. Believe me, it would survive.

I am a hockey purist. I think the shootout we have in hockey today is okay, as long as they don't put it in the playoffs. Personally, I don't like a team getting a point for just getting the game to the shootout stage. There is something not quite right about that. You either win or you lose. I understand the reasoning for it. It makes good business sense. It keeps all of the teams in the league closer in the standings and thus ticket sales keep moving. It prevents teams from being eliminated from the playoffs early on in the season. On the other hand, it's hard to deny that the shootout is exciting. Fans love to see breakaways or penalty shots. Now we get to see several of them if the game goes to a shootout.

I see a lot of marginal penalties called in today's game. There are far too many penalties called in games—at all levels. Some officials think that in order to be considered good, they have to call a lot of penalties. That is just simply wrong. A good official will call a penalty when the action has had an effect on the game. I still remember a game when referee Art Skov said to me, "Watch the holding, Nanne. Next time I will call it on you. You should get yourself a piece of rope." My hold had no effect on the game and I appreciated what was said to me. The non-call had perhaps more of an effect than a penalty for two minutes, because I still remember it. I say, let the players play the game unless the action means something to the game or obstructions are affecting its flow.

I have another great passion and it's movies. When I was on my recruiting tour at the University of Minnesota, I was staying in Minneapolis and went to nine movies in four nights. I love movies and I also like to read, especially history. I am fascinated by it. When I travel, I am interested in the history of the area. I recall in the mid-1980s wanting to share some of my knowledge about history with some friends. I made arrangements for some of my general manager colleagues, Cliff Fletcher and Harry Sinden, to go to Rome when we were at the Olympic Games. We took a side trip on a day that there were no hockey games.

We went to the Vatican and toured the Basilica. It was wonderful exploring the old ruins and we were having a great time. As the three of us walked down the steps of the Basilica, a little Italian guy came running toward us with his arms up and yelling, "Louie, Louie, Louie Nanne. Louie Nanne!!!" It was amazing. I didn't know how he recognized me. It turned out he had once lived in Toronto and had gone back to Italy. He was a hockey fan and watched the Leafs all the time. It was fun talking to him. But the guys I was with, well, they didn't believe it. To this day they still think the whole thing was a set up. Cliff still believes I paid him $20.

• • •

It bothers me when too much pressure is put on young kids playing hockey. First and foremost, the youngster should be playing the sport to have fun. I understand parents' desire to see their children succeed, but you have to make it an enjoyable experience for the kids. Sports are entertainment. For kids, sports need to be presented as recreation, a time to enjoy it and learn about the game. The more fun they have, the harder you will see them work.

In my mind, it is critically important that kids do not lose the love of the game and the competitive spirit because of pressure put on them by their parents. It is very easy for a parent to become so wrapped up in their child that they don't realize their actions have harmful effects.

Both coaches and parents should pledge that everyone on the team gets an equal opportunity to play until they get to high school. Scotty Bowman put it best at a youth hockey clinic. He was asked whether he would play his best kids on the power play in tight situations.

Scotty felt that kids who were in bantams or below need to play. Period. He said, "You pick them, you play them. All of them."

Some kids are not as good as others, and some take longer to mature and develop their skills but they all should play. For kids today, hockey costs a lot of money and takes an incredible amount of parental time, so everyone needs an equal chance. No one should ever be short-changed in the process.

It is also important for kids to learn to play at all positions. This gives the young players an understanding of the complete game. It helps their defensive play and also helps them understand what their own teammates will be doing in different situations. Gump Worsley, one of the greatest goalies of all time, didn't play one game in the nets until he was 14 years old. The developmental level of kids varies so much. Phil Esposito didn't make the Junior A team until he was 19 years old—and he became one of the greatest scorers in NHL history! I tell coaches all the time that I understand how much they want to win, but I emphasize how important it is for kids and their development.

Right up through the bantam level, kids should play and become familiar with all five positions in hockey. They need to learn the game from every position. By doing this, they will understand all parts of the game and there will come a time when the player and the coach will figure out where the individual plays the best. But until that occurs, they should have fun experimenting at all the positions.

Today I can actually enjoy the game, even if my team doesn't win. I still enjoy watching the Wild or the Gophers play, regardless of the score. How can you not marvel at the speed, skill, and contact that you see?

I was recently at one of my grandson's games and they lost a very close game. Afterward, the coach says to me, "Lou, that was a tough game to lose."

I told him, "Yeah, but it was a great game to watch! You guys did so many good things on the ice. It was a pleasure to watch you play and see the outstanding way that you executed things, and to see how proficiently you played."

I have learned, now that I am out of the pressures and the bright lights, to enjoy the game and not worry about the wins and losses. It has taken me a long time to get there but it is a joy to experience. For example, I am a die-hard Vikings fan. Every year I want them to win the Super Bowl, and when they don't I am disappointed. Naturally, I was quite disappointed when they lost to New Orleans last season! But then I remind myself of the fact that they had a great season and were a terrific team, and what a great time I had watching them all year. It helps.

In sports today, free agency has really changed the game. When I was playing, I never wanted to be traded; I never wanted to play for other any team but the North Stars. Some of the greats of all time stayed with their team for 20 years or more and became legendary in their home city. Today a player might play for as many as five or more teams before his career is over. There is no stability, no loyalty. Players who spend their career in one city are the exception, not the rule. Fortunately you do get a Yzerman or a Modano every now and then who remains with the franchise.

I had some significant injuries in my career like many others. Some happened when I got in the way of a puck or stick, and some of the injuries were brought about by my relentlessness to win at all costs. I had three concussions in my career. One night I hit my head on the ice in Pittsburgh and wound up with seven stitches under my helmet. I tried to get up and I couldn't. I had never been carried off the ice before that night. I don't remember much about it, but I do remember Tom Reid, my defense partner and current color analyst for the Wild, saying to me as I went back down, "Hey, Louie, before you go, can I have your condo in Florida?" I was back on the ice two days later.

One of my very first injuries was in Los Angeles. They had a big, strong guy named Larry Cahan. He started coming up the ice and I thought, *I am going to really lay it to this guy.* I thought I was a good body-checker and I was sure I could hit him pretty hard. When I hit him, I separated my shoulder. It hurt so much, I couldn't even lift my arm.

My second shoulder injury came against Toronto. I went behind the net and got blasted by Brian Glennie, crashed into the boards, and dislocated the same shoulder. This was on a Saturday night. By our next game, on Wednesday, our trainer had devised a device that would hold my arm up so I could play. He made it out of some kind of special material that he got from the Vikings.

Sometimes you don't know how badly you are hurt. One night in L.A. I stopped a slap shot with my ankle. Afterward we flew to Vancouver for our next game. In the morning I went to the doctor to see if my ankle was cracked. The doctor told me it was just a bruise but the crack on the other side of the ankle was healing nicely. I didn't even know I had a crack there! Then again, it wasn't really a surprise.

I also had knee problems and had to do a lot of taping through the years. Doc Rose was our trainer with the National and Olympic teams before he joined us with the North Stars. He was a huge help to me. Before every practice and every game he would tape my leg, put an Ace bandage around it, and then I would put a brace over the top. This kept me playing at times when I couldn't even walk properly.

I also recall a real elbow problem that developed after I received a cut and had it stitched up. Every time I played a game, it would open up and I would get it stitched again. It was playoff time and it continued through the weeks. In May I went on the USO tour to

Vietnam and my elbow was still a mess. There was a big knob on it, and if I bent it, pus would run out of the sore. It was awful.

When we returned home, I went to the doctor and they discovered that the last time they stitched it up, they had sewn part of my elbow pad into the wound—so it had just kept festering for weeks.

I stopped counting the amount of stitches I had on my face after I got to 320. Most of the injuries came from sticks, pucks, and elbows. One night the Olympic Team was playing the Soviets and I took a slap shot right over the eye. Fortunately my prominent forehead takes most of the blows so I could typically just stitch up and go back to the ice.

I had broken my nose many times before that night in Boston when I took a puck right in the nose. That night, I was taken to the hospital and the team was going to Philadelphia to play the next game. The doctor wanted me to spend the night while they worked on my nose. That was going to be a problem because I had a gift certificate from Bond Clothing Store in Philly, and it was about to expire. So I told the doctor that I had to be on the team plane that night and to do what he had to do. He put a bar up my nose and moved it a few times. I thought rockets were going off in my head but it sure looked straighter to me. I got to Philly and used that certificate and returned with a beautiful blue dress coat.

In my hockey career, I was fortunate to have won some prestigious awards. They have always meant a lot to me. One of my biggest honors is the Lester Patrick Award that I won in 1989. This award is presented by the National Hockey League and USA Hockey to honor a recipient's contributions to the game of hockey in the United States. It was an incredible feeling. After all, I was a Canadian kid who came down from Sault Ste. Marie and never knew what life had in store. I loved my involvement with USA Hockey. I thoroughly enjoyed being involved with hockey at all levels and am very happy to try and improve the opportunities for kids who came after me. I will treasure the award for the rest of my life. It has really meant a lot to me.

The Lester Patrick Award reminds me of the night I was in New York for the ceremony. A guy named "Snooks" was speaking. All of the speakers were given four or five minutes, so the speeches were short—but Snooks went on and on for a half an hour. Finally a man in the audience of a thousand people gets up and walks out. Just before he got to the door, he stops and hollers out, "Hey, Snooks, when you are finished, turn out the lights." It brought the house down.

I have been able to broadcast, play, and manage for more than 40 years. And now, as the years pass and I move farther away from the professional game, I still have the opportunity to express my passion and love for the game from the broadcast booth at the State High School Hockey Tournament. This year was a special time when I called the game involving my grandson, Lou Nanne. It was a bonus that the Edina Hornets won the state championship. Now I get to look forward to see if Vinny Lettieri, Michael Nanne, and Tyler Nanne will also get an opportunity to experience it.

As you look back on the highlights of your life, there are so many memories. Some of them are wonderful and other times you have to question why things happen as they do. Your faith gets tested and you realize the importance of your family and God in your life. We learned this with Michael's motorcycle accident many years back. I learned the importance of family and how there was nothing in my life that I wouldn't have given up to keep Michael alive. He survived the accident and has been an inspiration to our whole family and to many others who have suffered similar fates.

Now we are being tested again and wonder what God has in store for us and Michael. He has recently been diagnosed with a brain tumor and has undergone therapy. Like always, he is the one keeping everyone else's outlook positive. He is an amazing person. We don't know what the future holds for Michael—or any of us, for that matter. But it is part of the journey that we travel. I am forever thankful that I have been able to share it with my family.

The time has flown by but the memories, friendships, and experiences remain. I often think about my good fortune and realize how blessed my life has been. For the most part, it has truly been a challenging and interesting ride. I am grateful that I had the opportunity to share it with you. Thanks for joining me.

Co-Author's Note

I first heard the name Lou Nanne when he started playing hockey at the University of Minnesota in the early 1960s. Lou was a tremendous player for the Gophers and when he captured the WCHA scoring title as a defenseman, I remember thinking what an incredible achievement it was.

From the university, I followed his dynamic career as a player with the U.S. Olympic Team, the Minnesota North Stars, and later as the team's general manager and president. I remember my mother-in-law writing a letter to him because she was upset at something the North Stars were doing, and I was very impressed when she got a call back from Lou to discuss her concern. It meant a lot to her.

Of course, I have watched Lou and listened to his analysis and color commentary of the Minnesota State Boys High School Hockey Tournament for the past 46 years, but I never had the opportunity to get to know him until we started working on his autobiography together.

It would be an understatement to say that the past several months have been a wonderful experience. Lou Nanne is one of the most colorful and interesting personalities one could ever meet. I found him to be thoughtful, caring, concerned, and humorous. In fact, adjectives describing his personality alone would fill books and library shelves.

My initial concern of being sure we captured everything in his life for the book was discarded early on in the process, when I realized there was not a remote chance that could happen. There is more to this man's life and personality than I could have imagined.

Lou Nanne is one of the most internally driven individuals I have met in my life. He has been a success at everything he touches. He was an extremely talented hockey player and administrator, and he is deeply devoted to his family, the most important thing in his life. He ended one marvelous career and has solidified another in competence and brilliance.

Each path of his remarkable journey, from playing hockey on the streets of Sault Ste. Marie to championing the Olympic Team, the North Stars, and the world of finance, has been filled with wonderful stories, anecdotes, messages, humor, and an overwhelming desire to succeed. Few people are afforded the human qualities incorporating the passion, dedication, commitment, and effort of a Lou Nanne. Lou not only possesses these strong features within his character but employs them at a level few are able to attain.

In talking with his many friends in his hockey and personal life, I found that they all say basically the same thing about Lou, they just express it differently. Within each, Lou is described with attributes and qualities worthy of the highest esteem. He is revered for his friendship, humor, passion, dedication, and loyalty. His friendship is forever and his deep caring and concern for others is eternally blessed.

It has been an honor for me to work with Lou on his book. There has never been a dull moment on our journey. He has been inspiring, creative, and honest to a fault. When it comes to honesty, integrity, and credibility, he walks the walk and talks the talk. I feel fortunate to have been there with him.

I have had the privilege few others have had. I had the opportunity to work with Lou Nanne for many months to tell his life story in this autobiography. He has told it leaving no stone unturned.

And for me, maybe the best of all is being able to call him my friend.

—*Jim Bruton*

Afterword

Dad has always given 110 percent to everything he does. For years he committed his time and energy to his career, first as a hockey player and then as an executive running the team for the Minnesota North Stars. His passion and competitive drive brought the team from mediocrity to the Stanley Cup Finals in 1981. He also devoted many hours toward USA Hockey, which has played a big part in his life ever since he became an American citizen in 1967 in order to play in the 1968 Olympics for the United States.

His desire to be the best at everything he does transferred from sports into the business world in 1994. He still has not learned how to take no for an answer.

Dad has always been a role model for us, demonstrating that nothing comes easy and that you have to be passionate about what you do. His willingness to help people and to always be the one to get things done has never wavered. He is always up for a challenge. He has utilized this trait to help many causes, but especially fundraising for the University of Minnesota. He bleeds maroon and gold and has never once said no when it comes to helping raise money, recruit coaches, or persuade those who have chosen to sit on their hands to get up and devote time and money to the institution that was so influential in their lives.

He has been an amazing father and grandfather to us four children and his 11 grandchildren. He has taught us that family always comes first, to stand by each other, and to always support one another. He is happiest when the whole group of 21 is together, whether it is at home or in Italy at some great villa telling stories and drinking wine.

We are so proud of all our father's accomplishments—too many to mention. However, we think his best accomplishment was in marrying the most beautiful, caring, giving, supportive, loving person in the world: our mother, Francine. Mother, you have done more for Dad than you will ever know. We are so proud of you for molding Dad into the person he is and us into the people we are. You are amazing.

Dad, we love you so much and we are very proud of you. We look forward to many more special family times together.

Sincerely,

Michelle

Mike

Marc

Marty

Appendix

Lou Nanne
by the Numbers

NHL CAREER STATISTICS*—REGULAR SEASON

Season	Age	Team	GP	G	A	PTS	PIM
1967–68	26	Minnesota North Stars	2	0	1	1	0
1968–69	27	Minnesota North Stars	41	2	12	14	47
1969–70	28	Minnesota North Stars	74	3	20	23	75
1970–71	29	Minnesota North Stars	68	5	11	16	22
1971–72	30	Minnesota North Stars	78	21	28	49	27
1972–73	31	Minnesota North Stars	74	15	20	35	39
1973–74	32	Minnesota North Stars	76	11	21	32	46
1974–75	33	Minnesota North Stars	49	6	9	15	35
1975–76	34	Minnesota North Stars	79	3	14	17	45
1976–77	35	Minnesota North Stars	68	2	20	22	12
1977–78	36	Minnesota North Stars	26	0	1	1	8
Career		11 Seasons	635	68	157	225	356

*GP: games played / G: goals / A: assists / PTS: points / PIM: penalties in minutes

NHL CAREER STATISTICS—PLAYOFFS

Season	Age	Team	GP	G	A	PTS	PIM
1969–70	28	Minnesota North Stars	5	0	2	2	2
1970–71	29	Minnesota North Stars	12	3	6	9	4
1971–72	30	Minnesota North Stars	7	0	0	0	0
1972–73	31	Minnesota North Stars	6	1	2	3	0
1976–77	35	Minnesota North Stars	2	0	0	0	2
Career		5 Seasons	32	4	10	14	8

MINNESOTA NORTH STARS—TEAM STATISTICS

Season	Nanne's Position	W	L	T	PTS	Finish	Playoffs	Coaches
1967–68	Player	27	32	15	69	4th	Lost NHL Semi-Finals	W. Blair (27-32-15)
1968–69	Player	18	43	15	51	6th		J. Muckler (6-23-6)
1969–70	Player	19	35	22	60	3rd	Lost NHL Quarter-Finals	W. Blair (9-13-10), C. Burns (10-22-12)
1970–71	Player	28	34	16	72	4th	Lost NHL Semi-Finals	J. Gordon (28-34-16)
1971–72	Player	37	29	12	86	2nd	Lost NHL Quarter-Finals	J. Gordon (37-29-12)
1972–73	Player	37	30	11	85	3rd	Lost NHL Quarter-Finals	J. Gordon (37-30-11)
1973–74	Player	23	38	17	63	7th		J. Gordon (3-8-6), P. MacDon-ald (20-30-11)
1974–75	Player	23	50	7	53	4th		J. Gordon (11-22-5), C. Burns (12-28-2)
1975–76	Player	20	53	7	47	4th		T. Harris (20-53-7)
1976–77	Player	23	39	18	64	2nd	Lost NHL Preliminary Round	T. Harris (23-39-18)

*GP: games played / G: goals / A: assists / PTS: points / PIM: penalties in minutes / T: ties

Season	Nanne's Position	W	L	T	PTS	Finish	Playoffs	Coaches
1977–78	Coach/ General Manager	18	53	9	45	5th		T. Harris (5-12-2), A. Beaulieu (6-23-3), L. Nanne (7-18-4)
1978–79	General Manager	28	40	12	68	4th		H. Howell (3-6-2), G. Sonmor (25-34-10)
1979–80	General Manager	36	28	16	88	3rd	Lost NHL Semi-Finals	G. Sonmor (36-28-16)
1980–81	General Manager	35	28	17	87	3rd	Lost Stanley Cup Finals	G. Sonmor (35-28-17)
1981–82	General Manager	37	23	20	94	1st	Lost NHL Division Semi-Finals	G. Sonmor (37-23-20)
1982–83	General Manager	40	24	16	96	2nd	Lost NHL Division Finals	G. Sonmor (22-12-9), M. Oliver (18-12-7)
1983–84	General Manager	39	31	10	88	1st	Lost NHL Conference Finals	B. Mahoney (39-31-10)
1984–85	General Manager	25	43	12	62	4th	Lost NHL Division Finals	B. Mahoney (3-8-2), G. Sonmor (22-35-10)
1985–86	General Manager	38	33	9	85	2nd	Lost NHL Division Semi-Finals	L. Henning (38-33-9)
1986–87	General Manager	30	40	10	70	5th		L. Henning (30-39-9), G. Sonmor (0-1-1)
1987–88	President/ General Manager	19	48	13	51	5th		H. Brooks (19-48-13)
1988–89	President	27	37	16	70	3rd	Lost NHL Division Semi-Finals	P. Page (27-37-16)
1989–90	President	36	40	4	76	4th	Lost NHL Division Semi-Finals	P. Page (36-40-4)

*GP: games played / G: goals / A: assists / PTS: points / PIM: penalties in minutes / T: ties

Other Career Statistics

Season	Age	Team	League	GP	G	A	PTS	PIM
1960–61	19	University of Minnesota	WCHA	30	4	12	16	52
1961–62	20	University of Minnesota	WCHA	22	4	11	15	37
1962–63	21	University of Minnesota	WCHA	29	14	29	43	30
1965–66	24	Rochester Mustangs	USHL	25	23	22	45	4
1966–67	25	Rochester Mustangs	USHL	24	11	12	23	8
1967–68	26	United States	Olympics	7	2	2	4	12
1968–69	27	Memphis South Stars	CHL	3	0	1	1	0
1968–69	27	Cleveland Barons	AHL	10	1	2	3	8
1975–76	34	United States	WEC-A	10	1	3	4	26
1976–77	35	United States	Can-Cup	5	0	2	2	6
1976–77	35	United States	WEC-A	10	2	2	4	19

*GP: games played / G: goals / A: assists / PTS: points / PIM: penalties in minutes

About the Authors

After **Lou Nanne** captained the Minnesota Gophers and the United States Olympic hockey teams, he had a remarkable tenure as player, coach, general manager, and president of the Minnesota North Stars. Since his retirement from professional hockey he has championed a successful occupation in the financial industry. He resides in Edina, Minnesota.

Coauthor **Jim Bruton**, a former prison warden, is the author of *The Big House, A Tradition of Purple, Every Day Is Game Day,* and *Gopher Glory*. Bruton was a member of the Minnesota Golden Gophers football team in 1965 and 1966 and signed professional football contracts with the Minnesota Vikings and the Dallas Cowboys.